The Salad Garden

The Salad Garden

Elisabeth Arter

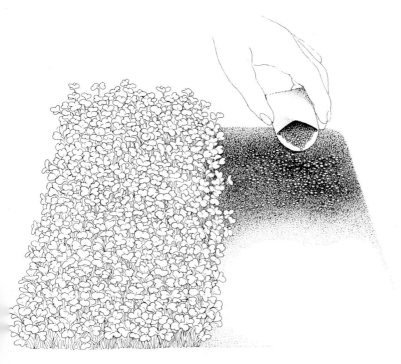

CROOM HELM
London & Canberra

©1984 Elisabeth Arter
Croom Helm Ltd, Provident House, Burrell Row,
Beckenham, Kent BR3 1AT
Croom Helm Australia Pty Ltd,
28 Kembla Street, Fyshwick, ACT 2609, Australia.

British Library Cataloguing in Publication Data

Arter, Elisabeth
The salad garden
   1. Vegetables   2. Salad gardens
   I. Title
   635'.5   SB322

ISBN 0-7099-0530-0

Line drawings by David Henderson

Typeset by Columns of Reading
Printed and bound in Great Britain

Contents

Illustrations

Introduction

There are so many ways of serving a salad, and so many ingredients you can blend in to vary flavours and colours, that it is possible to produce something different for every day of the year.

So often I've seen foreign tomatoes and cucumbers, flabby heartless lettuces and the salad rape that masquerades these days for mustard and cress, as though they were the only choice of salad material in most months. A few years back the greengrocery shelf at the supermarket would have been stocked with little else; but now I find there is an increasing variety of ingredients that can be served raw. If you browse around in the supermarkets, and in the smaller or more selective greengrocers, you can find many plants to make your salads more exciting, even during the winter months. But, for really interesting salads, you need to grow as many plants as you can at home – for that way you can have the widest possible choice at all times and can serve everything in tip-top condition straight from the garden.

For me, preparing a salad requires the same technique as flower arranging. For that, I like to stroll round the garden with a pair of secateurs to gather a bloom here and a bit of foliage there to create a symphony of colour for the house. For a salad, I like to wander round with a pair of kitchen scissors, a sharp knife and a colander to collect pieces of this and that to make a mixture that will look good, taste good and be full of goodness. Even in mid-winter I can generally find many different plants to use.

I'm all for growing at home; one of the big advantages is that you can produce a far wider selection of varieties than is available from the commercial growers who must stick to the heavy-yielding, best-selling crops that travel to market well and appeal to the housewife. They must rely on the 8-to-a-lb tomatoes, though anyone who has experimented with the small, bite-sized varieties or those with yellow and stripy skins

1

knows that they taste just as good. Those butterhead cabbage lettuces beloved by the market growers are all very well, but I like to serve too the big summer cos, those sweet 'Little Gem' that need so little room, the crunchy crisphead 'Webbs Wonderful'-type and the loose leaf cut-and-come-again varieties.

Growing Your Own

What you grow at home must, of course, be governed by the size of your garden. However, a lot of salad stuffs can be fitted into a tiny plot and I find some of the most exciting demand very little growing space. Rely on the shops for cabbage, maincrop carrots and celery in winter and you can vary the salads made from those basic ingredients by using all kinds of interesting plants from your own garden. In summer there is far more available, but then too it is more important to grow at home those plants you seldom see in the shops, or which need to be used immediately after gathering.

Go through the seed catalogues, including those of the firms that specialise in out-of-the-ordinary vegetables – perhaps from Europe or the Orient – and you'll discover some exciting plants that you are very unlikely to encounter in the shops. In fact, you are unlikely to find seeds of many of them in the average garden shop, because they too think only in terms of the bestsellers.

Every cook needs a herb bed and though lots of these plants are used more often in cooked dishes, many of them are very good served raw in small amounts. Used with discretion, herbs add a variety of flavours to pep up the more mundane items we use for salad bases and between them have many health-giving properties.

The flower garden will provide various petals to add colour, seeds to add flavour and leaves to add both. Some of our wild plants can be included on the salad list too, but you must be very sure no herbicides or insecticides have been applied in the vicinity before gathering any bits from the countryside. If there is a native plant you want to use regularly, I'd advise growing a plant or two in the garden where you know it will not be contaminated by chemicals or traffic fumes.

To keep up a good supply of fresh salad stuffs through winter you need some protection for garden plants. Cloches or a cold frame are invaluable, but the keen gardener needs a greenhouse for maxium protection in the cold months and for starting seedlings into growth early in spring. Compare prices with a generation ago and you will find that greenhouses are far cheaper today than then. In 1957, I paid £56 for a 12 x 8 ft cedarwood house and the same today would cost several hundred pounds, but that is nothing like the increase that you find in wages or in houses prices between then and now. Mass production, the universal use of aluminium and greater demand from home gardeners have brought greenhouses within the reach of us all. But, don't despair if you have no glass or polythene to protect the crops in your garden, for you can do a surprising amount in a sun lounge or on sunny windowsills to start off spring crops and overwinter herbs.

Containers are the answer when garden space is very restricted and salad devotees will go to great lengths to devise the most ingenious methods to raise crops in window boxes, tubs and pots. But perhaps the greatest boon of all, both for the greenhouse and for courtyard gardening, is the growing bag filled with a peat-based mixture. The bag should never be used for similar crops more than once, but can take two or three crops if unrelated plants unlikely to be affected by the same pests and diseases are chosen. Use a bag for summer tomatoes or cucumbers and then follow on with winter lettuce or other saladings and use early carrots for a third crop in spring.

Salads do take a bit of time to prepare, but there is little or no time lost in cooking, and they are so useful when meals have to be staggered because different members of the family come in at different times. And salads are the easiest of all things to go in packed meals – and taste so very much nicer than sandwiches.

Preparing Your Salads

If you are prepared to spend a bit more time in preparation, salad stuffs can make tempting and tasty party titbits. If you like entertaining you can enjoy yourself in thinking up unusual party snacks with some of the less usual salad ingredients, that may surprise your guests. At one time or another most of us have been served lengths of celery stalk filled with cheese spread, radishes cut into waterlily shapes, or bits of cucumber cut round the edges so they are deeply serrated. Rather more exciting are 'Sweet 100' bite-sized tomatoes served whole on cocktail sticks along with the usual miniature sausages; slices of dessert apple dipped in lemon juice to preserve their colour and topped by cheese spread and chopped chives or nuts, or by salmon and cucumber; or small cracker biscuits spread with pâté or soft cheese topped by seeded and diced red pepper, raw green peas, slices of red 'Cherry Belle' radishes, tiny

Introduction

'Silverskin' onions, or peanuts and seedless raisins, and a garnish of very finely chopped herbs.

For every day, I use three different ways of serving a salad. One is to toss all the ingredients together in a big bowl to be served out as they come, often adding some chopped herbs or other extra as a garnish. Another is to arrange the different items in separate piles on a large platter, or in several dishes, so each person can choose what they fancy. The third is my favourite method, and consists of arranging a pile of shredded cabbage, some lettuce leaves, or other basic items, with the other ingredients placed on top – so each can be identified and they all blend together both for eating quality and good looks. If you prefer individual servings, the same methods can be adapted for smaller plates.

So many people dislike the thought of packed meals because they associate them with dreary sandwiches, but prepare a lunch box with a selection of whole salad items, or fill a soft margarine tub with a blend of grated and chopped salad stuffs, and pack a crusty roll and butter, some cold meat, cheese or hard-boiled eggs and whatever you fancy to follow – and those with a packed lunch will eat as well as those at home.

For some people, salads are very much a part of the summer menu, and salads are no longer served once the days shorten. But, with carefully chosen ingredients, they can be just as interesting through the cold months and are important then for maintaining health and warding off infection. If you don't like the idea of a completely cold meal, start off with hot home-made soup, serve salad with hot meat, or with cold meat and a jacket potato straight from the oven.

In my recipes, I've concentrated mostly on vegetable ingredients, assuming that the salad will be served to accompany a main dish. I have sometimes, however added cheese or one of the other proteins; for garnish, I usually rely on chopped herbs, nuts, fresh or dried fruit, or flower petals.

Salad stuffs are full of goodness – most plants are far more nutritious when eaten raw, and rapidly lose vitamins once they start to cook. Crunchy vegetables and fruit help to maintain clean, healthy teeth and raw foods are splendid for slimmers, though anyone watching calories should beware of fattening salad dressings. Use plenty of interesting plants to make your salads, and you won't want to smother them and disguise their flavours with mayonnaise!

Shop well, grow well and serve well – and I don't think

anyone will complain because salad is on the menu, whatever
the date and whatever the weather.

CHAPTER 1

Lettuce

However much you like to make use of unusual and exotic ingredients for your salads, lettuce is bound to be your number one choice through most of the year.

Historical Background

The lettuce has been enjoyed since very early times and it is thought to have been brought to Britain by the Romans. The name is derived from the Latin *Lactuca* and the Saxons called the plant lactuce, while in the fifteenth century a gardener's book referred to it as letows.

Today we know that lettuce is a valuable source of the vitamin C that helps ward off colds and winter chills and ills and maintains fitness; while it also contains protein, calcium, iron and potassium as well as dietary fibre. Our forebears did not know that, but they appreciated its health-giving properties, believing among other things that eating lettuce for supper helped give a good night's sleep. My grandmother reckoned that the central stem was specially good for inducing sleep and if ever we had a row that was running up to seed, she would choose herself a good-sized bit of the developing stem for her supper. Some old folk recommended lettuce juice mixed with oil of roses for applying to the forehead of the sick and weak who needed sleep and I've also seen this recommended for easing headaches.

Buying Lettuce

If you have to buy from the shops, lettuce is obtainable all year round, though for much of the time supermarkets will offer only the rather boring round cabbage varieties that do not always heart up well. You will do much better if you can patronise greengrocers or market stalls which buy in small quantities from small growers not so reliant as the big commercial producers on the most conventional varieties. For the freshest nicest lettuce and a better choice look out for

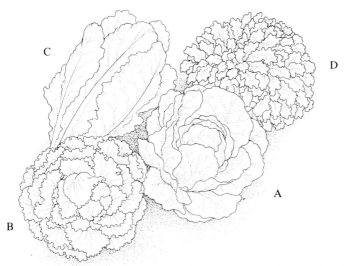

Figure 1: Different types of lettuce: (A) butterhead, (B) crisphead, (C) cos, (D) loose leaf

gardeners offering produce for sale from their homes. That way I've found some deliciously fresh lettuce at very modest cost. Very often garden-gate heads will be cut while you wait and small shops may well have a supply brought in direct from the grower's land on the day of sale. When buying look for well-developed heads with tight full hearts, with leaves that are fresh and crisp. Avoid those with withered or discoloured outer leaves and those with outer leaves removed, as this could be a sign of stale lettuce.

Storing Lettuce

When you arrive home store lettuce for as short a time as possible either in the salad drawer of the fridge or wrapped in newspaper in a large saucepan with the lid on. Once washed, store in a polythene container in the fridge after allowing time to drain in a colander with leaves upright so water runs off readily. Drying in a tea towel or in a salad shaker will give bruised spoiled leaves with any of the softer varieties.

Using Lettuce

Serve lettuce hearts whole in salads or for packed lunches, and roughly tear up the outer leaves that are in good condition for the base of mixed salads – shredding with a knife damages the cells and leads to quick loss of goodness. A big leaf from a large summer cos or 'Webbs Wonderful' can be used as an attractive holder for a mixed salad and can be slid direct onto the plate at serving time. The cold weather lettuce that seldom hearts up properly is best torn up for mixed salads and so are the frilly leaves of the loose leaf summer varieties like 'Salad Bowl'. You can use them too for forming a ring of pretty greenness round the outside of a salad platter.

Use surplus plants from the seed row as leaf salads when fully grown lettuce are not available. I find it worth putting in a row in the cold greenhouse right at the start of spring especially to use as 2-3 ins-high leaves. These are gathered a handful at a time, leaving the base of the seedlings to send up new foliage for another picking, and a row will produce salad material over some weeks. Instead of sowing a row, you can broadcast seed over an area of up to a yard square to give a cut-and-come-again crop that's a very economical use of land. The big summer cos varieties like 'Lobjoits Green' are recommended for growing like this, but I usually use leftover seeds from packets that have already served me for two or three seasons.

I like to grow quite a few different lettuce varieties in the year, but don't outlay a great deal on seed because each packet will stay viable for at least three seasons and any approaching staleness are used up in this way.

Growing Your Own Lettuce

Growing at home allows the freshest possible lettuce and the widest choice of varieties. If you have relied on the supermarket or chain store you may not realise how many different types of lettuce there are on the market and that this alone can supply very different salads depending on which varieties are grown.

Even if you have only a very small garden it should be possible to grow some of your own lettuce, at least in the warmer months. If you have more room then this is one of the most important crops to grow, because freshness is so essential. It's also one of the main crops to go under cloches, in a cold frame or in the greenhouse border.

You can't freeze lettuce or preserve it in any other way, and as plants fairly soon run up to flowering after maturing it's silly to grow too many at one time. In fact, I've known people put off growing lettuce in the garden because they had nothing but a series of gluts and shortages all summer. I knew one thrifty housewife who swore by lettuce soup to cope with the over abundances, but that's not everyone's favourite dish and in my opinion is waste of a good salad crop.

The secret of being a good steady lettuce producer is to sow little and often, especially during the warmest months when transplanted seedlings have a nasty habit of bolting (running up to seed) rather than making hearts. You should achieve the right balance between too many and not enough by sowing a pinch of seed every two to three weeks from March to July.

Another secret is to grow on good fertile soil that has been deeply dug and generously enriched with organic matter, be it home-made compost or well-rotted farmyard manure. When preparing the site for a seed bed you'll generally need also to rake in a dressing of 2 ozs of general fertiliser to every sq yd of land, though this should be omitted from an autumn sowing or planting.

Particularly in summer, irrigation will be necessary to grow lettuce well, for they need ample moisture to develop quickly and satisfactorily. They dislike overhead watering, especially after hearts have started to form, and you'll do well to follow the example of the commercial growers who aim at really soaking the soil before planting to ensure that little more watering is needed.

To extend the season beyond the Easter to harvest festival period, when lettuce can be grown successfully in the open garden, you need some form of protection, and I find that inexpensive polythene tunnel cloches are just right. A cold greenhouse will extend the season even further and a warm house right into winter, but I find that a cold house and starting seedlings in the gentle warmth of an electric propagator or on a warm windowsill indoors proves satisfactory and costs very little.

Apart from the different types of lettuce, principally cabbage and cos, different varieties have been bred to mature at different times of year in different growing conditions and it is important to choose the right ones for your needs. Go through a good seed catalogue and you'll see that clear details are given of what to sow at each time.

I make my first sowing of the year early in January in a large seed pan or a seed tray covered by a plastic dome top or stood in a plastic bag and kept in a warm room until germination has taken place, using a cabbage butterhead variety like 'Suzan' or 'Fortune'. The cover is removed as soon as seedlings are nicely up and the pan or tray moved to a rather cooler place in full light to harden off a bit before the move out to my cold greenhouse. If there happens to be a particularly hard spell of weather the move is delayed, though there is a risk of this leading to drawn, leggy seedlings. Once in the cold house the baby lettuces are left for a few days to

9

develop further and then pricked out into seed trays – I favour Dutch tomato trays I've collected from a greengrocer because they are deeper than a standard seed tray and give more room for roots. Better still, especially if you need only a dozen or two plants, prick out seedlings into individual peat pots that will mean there is no root disturbance whatsoever when the plants are moved to their permanent place.

Some of my seedlings are grown on to go outside under tunnel clothes and others are planted out into the greenhouse border, doing specially well in a polythene tunnel house. Plants need at least 9 ins each way, but I tend to put them in at 6 ins either way and then cut alternate plants for leaf salads before they touch. That leaves 1 ft in both directions and allows for big lettuces to grow with firm hearts. Inside, it's particularly important not to water overhead and introduce damp and the resulting decay it can bring, so you need to soak the soil very thoroughly before planting. If plants are to go out under cloches, these will need to have been in position for a fortnight to warm and dry the soil.

I sow in the greenhouse border in February using the same variety to give a late spring succession and find that surplus from this row are super for cut-and-come-again leaf salads to eat before any hearted lettuce are ready.

Outdoor sowings can be made from early March, or you can use cloches for the first row and then go on to the open garden. For this I favour the quick-maturing sweet cos 'Little Gem', once known too as 'Sugar Cos', for this is the crispest, tastiest of all lettuce and is so compact that you need to thin to no more than 6 ins each way. Plants are almost all heart, with scarcely any outside rubbishy leaves.

The wild birds share my love of the sweet leaves and so plastic fruit netting or black thread stretched between sticks at each end of the row is vital to protect the young plants. So, I find, is slug killer put down in small amounts under bits of broken crock to avoid risk of pets or wild birds getting at it. In fact, this is something that needs to go down every couple of weeks through the summer if you want clean, undamaged salad leaves.

'Little Gem' can be sown in succession through to July and so can the crisphead 'Windermere', one of the 'Webbs Wonderful'-type raised by Suttons and Highly-commended by the Royal Horticultural Society in 1977. It has succulent crinkled leaves that stand up to more heat then the butterhead and cos lettuces and is one I like to use between May and early July. If you want a summer butterhead, 'Sigmahead', new from Suttons for 1981, makes good solid hearts at a close spacing and is good for March to June sowings.

If you like lettuce with a red tinge to the leaves to give a different look to your salad bowl, do grow the butterhead 'Continuity' for April to July sowings thinned and grown on *in situ*, but not transplanted – that means sowing thinly to avoid wasting precious seed.

Summer cos varieties like the new 'Barcarolle' give tall erect plants with long leaves of excellent flavour that make a splendid change from the different cabbage types. In their seed trials for 1979, Dobies reported heads yielding up to 1 lb of sweet crisp salading and so this is a real family variety.

For sowings between June and August I go back to the butterheads with 'Avondefiance', bred at the National Vegetable Research Station at Wellesbourne for resistance to the mildew that can be so trying with the late crop.

Loose leaf lettuce varieties are particularly valuable for sowing between June and August too, for they stand warmer weather than most hearted varieties and go on producing salading over a long period. I've picked tasty leaves from the same plants over a two-month period and that's a lot longer than ever I could from conventional varieties with solid heads. 'Salad Bowl' is the best-known loose leaf lettuce and for a variation Unwins offer a form with red leaves. I prefer the American 'Grand Rapids' with frilly leaves of excellent flavour – superb for tearing up as a salad base. You can also grow a

Figure 2: Cabbage lettuces in growing bag in greenhouse

11

summer cos like 'Lobjoits Green' for leaf lettuce, broadcasting seed over a square yard of good moist soil from which the first potatoes or some other early crop has been lifted. Cut leaves individually with a sharp knife so plants keep on producing more foliage and don't think of thinning unless plants are very overcrowded.

The last sowings of 'Little Gem', 'Avondefiance' and 'Grand Rapids' will give salad material for use all through October. To give lettuce for cutting in November and December under cold glass go for the butterhead variety 'Kwiek'. Sow seed at the end of August and you'll have plants to go in the border or empty growing bags immediately summer tomatoes or cucumbers are cleared at the end of September.

To produce lettuce for cutting in the first three months of the year you need heated glass and, as that's something few of us can afford these days, I'd advise buying from the shops or doing without until milder weather comes. However, for those with warm greenhouses there is the excellent variety 'Dandie' to sow in succession from August to November for cutting from November to April.

Not grown so much now as in the days before greenhouses were so universally popular, some lettuces can be sown in early September to overwinter in the open for spring cutting. 'Arctic King' was my grandfather's favourite because he found it so hardy and liked the compact heads of cabbage style. 'Winter Density' is a crisp tasty cos that does not stand up to so much hard weather, but is very very good to eat. Then there's the newer and larger cabbage variety 'Valdor' that should come through most winters completely unscathed with no protection of any kind. One old friend of mine always grew overwintering lettuce among his gooseberries, cutting for salads before the bushes came into leaf and thus producing two food crops from one bit of garden. I might add that friends and neighbours were only too pleased to share any surplus he was giving away in late April and early May.

If you are going to aim for lettuce over much of the year you will be anxious for all your sowings to grow away quickly, and early and late in the season I believe that makes some form of polythene or glass protection vital. In the summer it makes watering essential if you want to avoid those tough blue-tinged leaves that no one enjoys eating.

In the warm months you can speed germination and early growth by making sure the site is thoroughly moistened before preparing the seed bed and in very dry weather you will find it

Figure 3: Seed drill being lined with damp peat before summer sowing

helps if the seed drill is lined with damp peat before the seed is sown. Experiments at the National Vegetable Research Station have shown that afternoon sowings germinate better than those made earlier in the day because the temperature-sensitive stages of germination take place during the night while soil is cooler.

I've mentioned growing lettuce in the greenhouse border during the colder months, but you may have staging and no border. If that's the case you can grow in deep boxes or pots, or in growing bags. These must not be used more than once for tomatoes, or any other crop one after the other, but can take a series of two or three totally different plants. That makes them ideal for end of season or start of season lettuce after one summer of tomato or cucumber growing. They are superb too for those people who grow salads in a courtyard or on a balcony.

Use lettuce as a intercrop between slower maturing vegetables, perhaps growing an April sown row between rows of dwarf or runner beans that won't need maximum room for some time. Use them too as a catch crop on land intended for a later planting, perhaps growing early cloched lettuce on the site of a celery trench prepared in winter to take the half-hardy seedlings at the end of May.

Grow the different types of lettuce I have recommended and I don't think anyone in your family could complain of the same salad every day. In the past I think we relied too much on hearted lettuce, and though that's important for those neatly quartered hearts to serve on their own, or with tomato and cucumber, it's by no means necessary for providing a bowl of mixed salad for every day of the year. By all means aim to

13

produce as many firm solid heads as you can, but do be prepared to use thinnings, alternate three-parts grown lettuce when the row is not quite ready, or even odd leaves taken here and there to make sure your family have some salad during the leaner times. Tossed in with a mixture of other ingredients no one will realise you have a gap in supplies, but will compliment you on a non-stop production line through the season.

CHAPTER 2

Radishes

Radishes are not a main ingredient of any of my salads, but are superb for adding variety of flavour and colour to a mixture of other ingredients at almost any time of year.

Historical Background

Radishes were enjoyed by the ancient Egyptians, and by the Romans long before they conquered this country and perhaps brought the salad with them.

The roots were served as a stimulant before meat in Tudor times and we are told that gardeners of those days used fences of reeds rather like upright mats to keep off cold winds and help produce early radishes. Like the people from the first Queen Elizabeth's day, we know that the first early pulling of spring is the one that everyone likes best and so we use our modern forms of protection to hasten the sowings made while winter is still with us.

Buying Radishes

I must confess that I've never bought a radish from a shop, mainly because I've always found them so easy to grow at home, and because summer varieties are invariably sold in big bunches and I prefer to pull just a few at a time so they are really fresh when brought to table. You do occasionally see the big winter radishes on sale in specialist greengrocers, but again they are so easy to grow at home and need very little room. My introduction to these was from an old cottage gardener who found one row gave more roots than she needed and was only too willing to share some of her largesse with my family. I think you'll be more likely to find winter radishes and other less usual vegetables on sale at Women's Institute market stalls, or from gardeners selling produce from their homes, than from the shops.

Storing and Serving Radishes

If you do buy radishes, top and tail the summer kinds immediately you arrive home, wash and dry the roots and store in a plastic container in the fridge until needed. These small summer radishes are super for serving whole with cheese and wholemeal or rye bread for supper, or just with cheese as a starter for a meal. When you are entertaining they can be cut into fancy waterlily shapes, but for everyday eating serve them just washed and trimmed with about an inch of tops left on. I think round red radishes look more appetising with some top on and many people say that they find them more digestible when some leaf and stalk is eaten with the root. You will probably be able to buy the big winter varieties singly, but because roots are large and go a long way you will need to store what is left over from the first meal, in the same way.

Growing Your Own Radishes

You don't even need a garden to produce summer radishes, for they are quite easy to grow in a big flower pot of potting compost, or in a growing bag used for tomatoes or cucumbers the previous season. Either could be stood out in a back yard or on a balcony, and I know someone who says that he finds radishes do so well in containers that he never bothers to grow them in the open garden.

When I prepare a cropping plan for my vegetable plot I allow no space for radishes, using them as an intercrop or

Figure 4: Radish being pulled from a row, with parsley seedlings at first true leaf stage

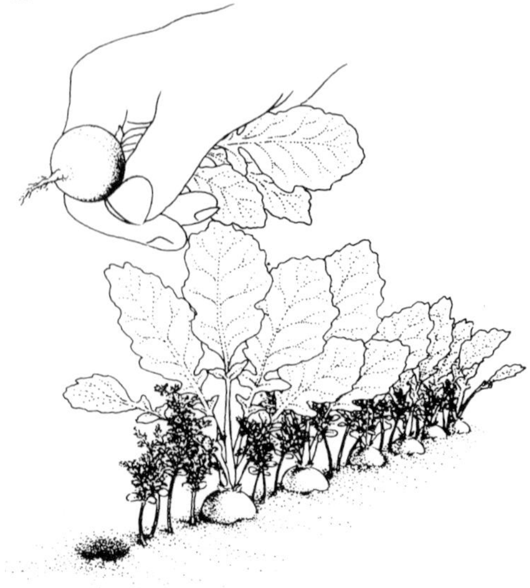

more often sowing the seed thinly along with some other slower growing crop in the same drills. I'll sprinkle a few 'Cherry Belle' or 'French Breakfast' seeds in the same drill as parsnips, parsley or other culinary crop that takes some weeks to germinate and develop to the true leaf stage. By then the quick-maturing radishes will have been pulled and eaten. I sow them too in drills with hardy annuals in the flower borders, finding the radish seedlings that pop up in about a week make splendid row markers and that their plump red roots are harvested before the little flower plants need much space.

As an intercrop a row of radishes can go between wider spaced rows of early potatoes or beans and peas to give roots for pulling far before the maincrop needs much light and room. When marrow or courgette plants go out in May I'll surround them with a ring of thinly sown radishes, both enjoying the same moist fertile conditions, and the roots will be eaten four or five weeks later while the main crop is still fairly small.

Right at the start of the season I'll sow radishes under cloches or in the greenhouse border between lettuce and other early salad or vegetable crops. Because the warmer conditions under protection tend to encourage leaf growth the seed goes in very thinly. This way there will be roots by Easter and from then on without a lot of trouble I'll be able to maintain a supply through to October.

Figure 5: Radish ready for pulling around developing courgette plant – in bloom, but not showing fruit

Radishes

The main secret of successful radish production is to sow little and often, because roots don't stay in tip-top condition for long once ready to pull, and to grow on fertile soil that's never allowed to become dry. I find radishes like clay and do better on heavy soil than on light land. They don't want fresh manure, but are better on ground well fed for the previous crop.

If you are not prepared to water it's a waste of time to sow the seed between May and July in most years, but given adequate irrigation radishes will grow quickly and superbly in hot weather. Plant them fairly near the house and use bowls of water from salad washing to irrigate the row, and there'll be no problem over maintaining production through a heatwave.

Figure 6: Grating a round 'Black Spanish' winter radish, with cylindrical 'China Rose' root lying nearby

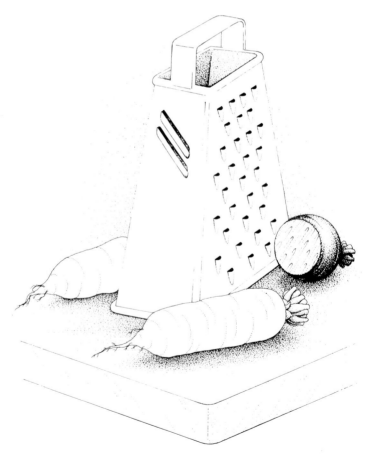

The round, bright-red, quick-maturing 'Cherry Belle' is one of my favourite varieties of summer radish; while I like the round, red 'Saxerre' for early growing under glass or polythene. The longer, cylindrical 'French Breakfast', with part red, part white roots, is splendid too and probably gives a heavier weight from the same length of drill. 'Icicle' is a good summer variety with long white roots, but doesn't look nearly as appetising as the red kinds.

Winter radishes are a much slower developing crop, but a very worthwhile one. Sow them in July on land from which an early summer vegetable has been harvested, making slightly deeper drills and sowing seed very thinly – one packet goes a long way, but can be kept for two or three seasons without losing viability.

Thin seedings to 2-3 ins apart and the big roots will be ready to pull from October. They can be left in the ground until the end of winter, but when hard weather threatens you need to protect the roots with a blanket of straw or other dry litter, or you can lift and store roots in a frost-free place in peat or dry sand. Never leave winter radishes in the ground after early March, as milder weather will make them run up to seed, but dig roots left then and store until needed.

The round 'Black Spanish' has ebony skin and white flesh and is best used at around golf ball size. 'China Rose' has bright rosy-red skin and white flesh and makes cylindrical roots about 5 ins long. Both have a far stronger flavour than their summer cousins, so you will find one root goes a long way. Best way to serve is very thinly sliced or grated. The Japanese 'Mino Early' has white skin and flesh and makes roots over 1 ft long that are more the size and shape of a parsnip. It is much milder, but even so I wouldn't recommend the variety for a couple or single person living alone, because one root would last too long.

There's no great food value in the radish, though some of the old folk used to believe that eating plentiful supplies would sweeten the blood and that they were good against the scurvy. But, they are an indispensable crop for salad lovers, so easy to grow at home and so good for serving whole, sliced or grated to add colour and complement the flavours of other ingredients in a salad. Use them too for serving alone, or in very small amounts to garnish mixed salads.

CHAPTER 3

Tomatoes

You are almost certain to use tomatoes as a main ingredient of your salads, but if you want to create exciting salads you won't always serve them in the same way and you won't always use the 8-to-a-lb round red tomatoes that commercial growers have to aim for.

In winter, when supplies must come from the shops you'll have to use these, but during the summer and autumn, when you can produce home-grown tomatoes, you can experiment with some of the less usual kinds. In the supermarkets and greengrocers you can also buy the large beefsteak tomatoes (so popular in Southern Europe), which have gained in favour over here during the past few seasons. These can be grown at home, however, together with the traditional medium-sized tomatoes; and the kinds with small sweet fruit that are super for serving whole or quartered in salads. For a change, you could try the yellow-fruited tomatoes and these look most effective when sliced and served with the red kinds.

Historical Background

They say that Christopher Columbus brought the tomato to Europe after finding the fruits grown by the Amerindians in Mexico and Peru and there's a record of the plants being grown in Britain in the mid-sixteenth century. For a couple of hundred years after that, tomatoes were grown as decorative plants or as a novelty and their fruits were treated with grave suspicion. After that, there was an idea that the fruit had an aphrodisiac quality and that was how they came to be called love apples, but I've not heard anyone suggest eating tomatoes for enlivening our sexual lives in the twentieth century.

It was during the last century that tomatoes began to be appreciated for salad use and it was realised that this was a valuable hothouse crop. Since then the plant has never looked back. We now know that the fruit is a good source of vitamin C and contains other important nutrients, as well as being one of the best-looking and tastiest salad stuffs. Indeed, it is estimated that in this country we eat an average of nearly ¼ lb each per week – and that's around two tomatoes come winter come summer.

When you buy tomatoes from the shops for salads look for firm ripe fruit with fresh green 'spider' calyces that prove they have not long been picked. For economy I sometimes also buy the over-ripe samples specially recommended for cooking and have found that though they are useless for serving whole or in elegant slices they cut up well in mixed salad and are very tasty. With these, I plunge the fruit first into boiling and then into cold water, so I can easily peel off the skins and cut them up well. For economy also look for extra large and small tomatoes, especially at the start and end of summer.

During summer you can often buy tomatoes from the farm gate, or from a gardener who has produced more than his family needs, and these will invariably be fresher and nicer than those from the shops.

A dish of sliced tomatoes is a salad in itself with only the need for a topping of chopped basil, chives or parsley leaves or some thin onion rings. Cut into small slices or pieces, quarters or wedges, the fruits blend well with all kinds of other salad ingredients and they look superb as a garnish for a salad made from green or creamy-green materials.

Unless you have a heated greenhouse, and few of us can afford that these days, producing tomatoes at home between Christmas and July is out of the question. It's not difficult though to maintain a supply from mid-July to the shortest day, and I'd say without a doubt that this is the most important crop for any cold or slightly heated greenhouse.

When growing at home, the plants can go out into a cold greenhouse around 16 April, so long as we are not in the middle of one of those arctic spells that sometimes occur in spring. It does help enormously if you can manage just a little heat at night for the first month, but even without that you should be picking fruit well before July is done. Plants have to be raised in warmth and I found buying them in rather costly, but for several years now have been very successful and saved quite an outlay by raising seedlings on windowsills indoors. In fact I've been able to pay for the seeds by selling surplus plants.

21

Figure 7: Pricking out tomato seedlings from a 3-4-ins flower pot into individual 3-ins black pots, 2-3 days after germination

I sow seeds in mid-February in a small pot of John Innes seed compost – that's a mixture of two parts by loose volume of sifted soil to one part each of sharp sand and peat. To each bushel of the mixture you should add 1^1_2 ozs of superphosphate; but when I'm making up just a tiny quantity to sow a few seeds I use loam from a fertile part of the garden and leave out the fertiliser. The pot is stood in a soft margarine tub that's kept filled with water until I can see that the surface of the soil is really moist, then surplus water is tipped away, the pot is covered with a plastic dome top and stood on our warm kitchen windowsill.

The seedlings emerge in a few days and as soon as the seed leaves have developed well, but before there is any sign of the true leaves, the infant plants are pricked out into individual 3-ins black plastic bag type-pots filled with John Innes potting compost No. 1 – that's a mixture of seven parts loam, three parts peat and two parts sharp sand plus 4 ozs of John Innes base fertiliser to every bushel. I mix my own at home, but you can buy the compost from a garden shop or centre. or, instead, you can buy the peat based soil-less composts, but

I've an idea that young plants are happier in soil.

The seedlings in their pots are grown on on different windowsills, gradually moving to cooler parts of the house until they are in the unheated utility room for a few days before the mid-April move to the cold greenhouse. Here they can go direct into the soil if you've a border, into large pots or other containers, or into growing bags.

The problem with growing in the greenhouse border is that there is a build up of root diseases if tomatoes are grown there for year after year, even if you change the topsoil. That's why I've gone over to growing bags and, although they are rather expensive, you can use them for other salad plants or herbs after the tomatoes have been harvested and when these are done use the contents of the bag to improve the soil in your garden, and so the cost need not be offset entirely against the tomatoes. I'm not going into full details of greenhouse tomato culture, for there are plenty of books on the subject, but will just say that the plants need regular, but not heavy, watering and liquid feeding from the time that the first truss of fruit has set.

Cold house tomatoes start to ripen around the middle of July and the main harvest is during August and September, but unless you are in a mad hurry to fill the house with chrysanthemums or some other autumn crop I find that late trusses will go on ripening a few fruits right up to Christmas, except in that exceptional year when we had severe frost early in December.

Completely in the open garden tomatoes are a chancy crop in our climate, but with protection from cloches, or when grown against a warm wall or some other sunny sheltered spot, they should do well. Here again you can make use of growing bags, the newer growing boards, or large flower pots and troughs.

I've heard it said that you should not attempt more than four trusses on staked outdoor tomatoes, but I knew one gardener who regularly produced and ripened six or more trusses. Every year he planted his tomatoes in a narrow border between the garden path and the south-facing brick wall of his cottage. They were staked with the type of taller pole usually used for runner beans and invariably grew to shoulder height. Although few other crops would have been happy in that restricted bed, the plants were fed regularly and given a mulch of lawn mowings that prevented the soil drying out and I never recall the fruits being affected by the blight which can be a curse with the outdoor crop.

23

Tomatoes

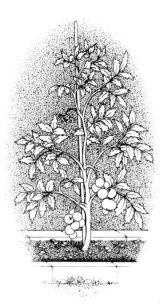

Figure 8: Tomatoes growing against a warm, outside wall, with mature fruit on lower trusses

You may not have such a good position as that, but with growing bags and other containers you can grow tomatoes against a warm wall that will reflect back heat even when there is no soil. Put them out in mid-May and use some kind of temporary plastic cover to assist an early getaway and you should be very successful.

You don't often see them now, but there used to be and probably still are available cloches made specially for tomatoes. They had flat tops which could be removed once the plants had reached 1 ft or so in height, and I know one gardener who uses them every year on a south slope where early ripening gives an outdoor harvest soon after the first fruits can be gathered from a greenhouse.

With the more usual types of cloches the best tomatoes are the dwarf bush varieties that need no staking or sideshooting, but need straw on the ground to protect ripening fruits from mud and dirt. Plant out under cloches in mid-May and either uncover once the tomatoes are reaching up to the top or, if there's room, leave the glass or plastic on for the whole season. 'French Cross' is an F_1 hybrid bush tomato from Suttons that crops heavily and makes such huge plants that they must be a good 2 ft apart. 'Alfresco' is another splendid variety and in trials plants have yielded 10 lb of fruit weighing 6-9 to the pound and of good eating quality apiece.

Figure 9: Different types of tomato fruit: (A) Plum-type, (B) Beefsteak, (C) 'Sweet 100', cherry-sized

I've advised putting outdoor plants in at the middle of May and that's fine if you can give some protection until frost risk is past, but if that's not possible it is wiser to delay planting until the end of the month. Seed for my outdoor planting goes in a pot on a warm windowsill at the end of March and plants are brought on in the same way as those for the greenhouse, but are given less warmth and are moved to the cold house early in May to harden off before going into the garden.

In a border, growing bags or in pots stood outside you can grow the taller varieties of tomato that we treat like cordons, removing all sideshoots so only the main stem grows up and bears fruit. Like the plants in the greenhouse they will need steady, but not too heavy, watering and will benefit from liquid feeding from the time that the first truss has set.

To prepare a site in the garden dig in winter and work in a good bucketful of garden compost or well rotted manure to every square yard, then rake in 3 ozs of general fertiliser per square yard before putting in the plants. For this outdoor crop 'Alicante' is a good variety of the traditional 8-to-a-lb type, which does well in soil or growing bags and will also do well in a cold house. Another dual-purpose variety, that's specially recommended for cold and slightly heated greenhouses but can also be grown outside, is the F_1 'MM'. This is similar to that old favourite 'Moneymaker', but unlike that is resistant to the leafmould (*Cladosporium*) that can be such a nuisance and also to greenback.

If you grow at home do try some of the big beefsteak tomatoes whose huge fleshy fruits are so good for slicing. The F_1 hybrid 'Big Boy' is good for the greenhouse, with firm red fruits of good flavour and quality that often weigh 1 lb each and may be twice that heavy. For outside I'd go for 'Super Marmande' that combines earliness, disease-resistance and enormous fruits.

At the other end of the scale come the bite-sized tomatoes, which are far more attractive when growing than traditional varieties. There's 'Sweet 100', an F_1 hybrid with big trusses carrying fantastic crops of inch-wide red round fruits; grow this outdoors and harvest until frosts come, or there's 'Gardeners Delight' that again produces long trusses with lots and lots of small sweet fruit, and is good for growing in pots on a patio or balcony.

We tend to think of tomatoes as red fruit, but some are yellow and they are fun to grow and serve in salads because they come as a surprise to most people. Recommended for growing outdoors, 'Yellow Perfection' is early and prolific with golden 8-to-a-lb size fruits.

If summer has been on the cloudy side, late September may well find you with green tomatoes left on the outdoor plants. These can be used like that for chutneys and pickles, but many can be ripened off if you strip leaves from the plants, remove

Figure 10: Ripening tomatoes indoors, by spreading out on cupboard shelf

stakes and lay the stems down on a carpet of straw under cloches. An alternative, and a method to adopt with any fruits that don't turn red after a few weeks under the cloches, is to gather the tomatoes, dry them off with a cloth and spread the crop out on a shelf in a warm cupboard indoors. Even the greenest fruits will eventually ripen, but you must check them over daily for any disease spores will rapidly multiply in the warmth of the house. The fruits ripened this way will be rather soft for serving whole, so are best chopped up well to blend into mixed salads.

You can't try all the varieties you want in a season and every year the seedsmen tempt us with new and interesting kinds. My advice is to aim at growing one of the traditional 8-to-a-lb tomatoes indoors or in the warmest spot you can find outside and then every year to experiment with at least one of the less usual varieties, choosing beefsteak, a yellow or one with lots of small sweet fruits. The best thing about growing tomatoes is that you don't need a garden to do so, but can be just as successful with a couple of growing bags or a few pots of John Innes against a warm sunny wall on a path, paved area or balcony.

CHAPTER 4

The Onion Family

To me, good mixed salad needs an onion flavour and there's seldom a day, when I don't use some member of the *Allium*, or onion, family. But that doesn't necessarily mean the 'White Lisbon' variety, that is pulled young and green and commonly referred to as the spring or salad onion. Of course, I grow and use that, but my salads include lots of other members of the family. Through winter we rely mainly on bulb onions, shallots and the so hardy leeks, but I use too the Welsh onions that should really be called everlasting onions. A perennial that's evergreen, these can make a splendid substitute for spring onions.

Chives covered over with cloches, grown in the greenhouse, or in a pot on a windowsill indoors will keep producing their grassy leaves through the cold months and these are excellent for adding a mild onion flavour and a finish to the salad bowl.

In spring all these are still available and there are also the first of the spring onions from an autumn sowing in the open or a late winter sowing under glass, together with thinnings from the bulb onions raised from seed sown in late summer. Before these are ready I'll bring in green tops and then salad onion substitutes from shallots planted in a pot in the greenhouse very early in New Year. So easy to produce, these are always a favourite early spring item for my family.

From Easter through to autumn there can be a supply of fresh salad onions if successional sowings of 'White Lisbon' are made in short drills every three or four weeks, and chives will keep up a steady supply of fresh 'grass' that's all the better for regular cutting.

Historical Background

Onions, shallots and leeks have been cultivated since ancient times and have been valued for their health-giving properties by peoples of many lands over many centuries. There's no particularly high vitamin content in the onion, but many older folk swear by it for helping ward off colds and winter chills, and that's a good reason for adding extra to cold weather salads. My mother loves raw onion and never enjoys a salad without a good helping of some member of the family and, though this may be a coincidence, she seldom catches cold. The leek does contain a good amount of vitamin C and has long been appreciated for medicinal properties, one old couplet running:

Eat leeks in March and wild garlic in May
Then all the year after physicians can play.

The leek is a native of Europe and is thought to have been brought to this country by the Romans, was widely cultivated in Saxon times and is, of course, the national emblem of Wales. One of the plant's great virtues is that it will stand any amount of cold and can always be guaranteed for fresh food at the end of a hard winter.

The onion is believed to have originated in Asia, has been cultivated in India since distant times and was eaten by the workmen who built the pyramids in Egypt. An important item in the British diet as far back as the Dark Ages, the onion is mentioned in a cookery book produced in the time of King Richard II. More recently, William Kitchener in his nineteenth-century *Cook's Oracle* wrote: 'All cooks agree in this saying, no savoury dish without an onion.'

I'd be inclined to add no salad without an onion, but there are some people who don't care for the flavour or who find the vegetable does not agree with them (That's one reason why I so often prepare salads in individual servings, so as to cater for onion lovers).

If you have to buy from the shops you'll be able to choose 'White Lisbon' through much of the year, leeks in autumn and winter, shallots for a few weeks of early autumn, and the big bulb onions at all times. But, for a continuous supply that gives a real variety and is readily to hand when needed, you have to grow at home. If space is restricted you can concentrate on the types that are seldom seen in the shops and just rely on them for the big bulbs and for bunches of spring onions. But, I'd hate to have to buy 'White Lisbon', as shop bunches are invariably too large to be eaten while all the onions are fresh. Growing at home allows you to pull just one or two at a time, so there's no need to store salad onions at all. It means also that you can use thinnings from varieties sown to

Buying and Storing Onions

29

produce big bulbs, again pulling only as many as you need for one meal.

If you do go to the shops for salad onions look for a bunch with leaves that are fresh and green and avoid those with yellowing outer leaves that obviously left the ground a good while back. Once home, trim off roots and outer leaves, wash well and store in the fridge in a plastic box until needed, keeping the onions away from other foodstuffs to avoid their acquiring an oniony flavour.

Growing Your
Own Onions

Spring or Salad Onions

Because the *Allium* family is extensive, I am going to go through growing methods for one type of onion at a time, dealing first with the 'White Lisbon'-type *spring onion* that everyone thinks of when salads are mentioned. But, this doesn't mean that I think it's of the greatest importance for eating raw.

A crop that demands little space, this will grow on any fertile soil that has been worked down to a fine tilth for seed sowing. Seed can go in drills in the open from early March to midsummer for use that season and again in August and early September, using the 'Winter Hardy' form, to overwinter in the open and pull early next spring. Don't sow more than a short row at a time and, during the spring and early summer, sow thinly so that no thinning is needed; for the first and last sowings allow rather more seed to make up for losses due to less favourable growing conditions.

Cloches will allow a February sowing if weather conditions are good and they have been positioned for a fortnight beforehand to warm and dry the seed bed. I like to sow in the greenhouse border then too, but if you have no border you can instead sow 'White Lisbon' in a growing bag used the previous summer for tomatoes or cucumbers. Kept weed free and well watered in dry spells, spring onions need no special care until they are ready for pulling.

In the kitchen they can be washed, trimmed of outer leaves and roots, and served whole or chopped in mixed salads. Some people throw away the green tops, but they are just as good to eat, and can be chopped to go in mixed salads to leave just the slim white part for serving whole.

Shallots

My next choice from the onion family for salad use is the
shallot, that's so easy to grow, so good green in spring, and
stores so well for winter eating.

Said to have been brought to Britain by the Crusaders in
the time of King Richard the Lionheart, the shallot is milder
than the big bulb onions and gives a high yield from a small
area of land, which is useful when you've only a small garden.

I believe that it's important to start off with a good variety
and worth paying a comparatively high price for the bulbs,
because you should always be able to save some of your crop
for planting next season and will seldom, if ever, need to buy
again. 'Giant Yellow' and 'Dutch Yellow' are the two varieties
you'll see offered by most firms, but I much prefer the large
flagon-shaped bulbs of the handsome 'Hative de Niort' that is
much favoured by those who grow for the show bench.

Shallot bulbs can be planted in the open garden in February
and March and they were sometimes put in at Christmas time,
but I see little advantage in such an early start. Like other
onions they like a good fertile soil and the ideal site is one
which, the previous autumn, was well dug and supplied with
well-rotted manure or garden compost. Choose a sunny open
spot and, as soon as the weather allows you to get onto the
garden, rake in a light dressing of general fertiliser and put the
bulbs in about 6 ins apart. Before doing so, I always snip off
the dried tops, as otherwise birds on the look out for nesting
material are inclined to pull them up before roots have
developed to give anchorage.

I plant my shallots with a narrow trowel, almost covering
the snipped off tops and then when the bulbs have started to
divide into the new season's shallots I gently ease away some
of the soil so they can spread out and develop more easily. If
I'm short of onion in spring, I'll snip off just a few of the green
shallot leaves to cut up and garnish a salad and if I've some
surplus shallots at planting time, I'll put in one row specially
for pulling as substitute salad onions at the stage when they've
just begun to divide. They are ready well before the first
sowing of 'White Lisbon' and are every bit as good to eat. The
shallots I've planted at New Year in a pot or in the border in
the greenhouse will be treated in just the same way, with first
the green tops coming in to chop as a garnish for my salads
and then the newly divided bulbs coming in as a splendid
substitute for spring onions.

Apart from weeding, the shallot row in the open garden

31

needs very little other care until the tops turn yellow and die down in July and the clusters of new bulbs are ready for gently lifting with a fork. Dry them off in the sun for ten days or so, rub off surplus skin and store in net bags hung up from a wire across the roof of a dry frost-free shed. 'Hative de Niort' produces far less bulbs in a cluster than the other varieties, but the bulbs are much larger and are of much higher quality. Before storing, all my shallots are sorted with any that are damaged or diseased put to one side for immediate kitchen use, often for chopping in our salads. Some of the best medium-sized bulbs are stored for next spring's planting, larger ones are saved for cooking and all the smaller bulbs for winter salad use.

Ripened off thoroughly, shallots store extremely well and will usually keep through to the following spring with no bother, though it is wise to check through the bulbs and remove any that look suspect every month or so.

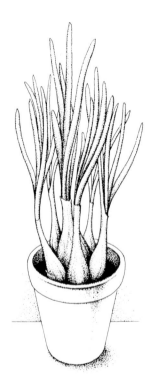

Figure 11: Shallots growing in flower pot, in greenhouse, at stage where they can be divided and used as substitute spring onions

Leeks

It was not until a couple of seasons ago that I discovered how good *leeks* are eaten raw, and now they are an important ingredient of our cold weather salads and can be relied on for that period of late winter when fresh salad stuffs are scarce and costly. The green tops are used in soups and that leaves the firm tender white stem for slicing in the salad bowl.

'Lyon-Prizetaker' is a good old variety of leek and 'Splendid' is a new one that sounds most promising. You can sow seeds in the open in early spring, but I like to sow mine in the greenhouse border or under cloches in February to give good pencil-thick plants for going out in June and early July as a follow on to cloched lettuce, earliest peas, or one of those other midsummer crops that thrive on land well supplied with organic matter in winter. Before planting, the land is given a light dressing of general fertiliser and holes 6 ins apart and 6 ins deep are made with a dibber, or a rake handle if you want to avoid too much stooping. Leek plants are lifted from a seed row that was well watered the night before so they come up easily, the roots and green tops are trimmed back by half and they are dropped into the planting holes; these are watered with no rose on the can and there's no need to fill in with soil.

Towards the end of summer many gardeners draw some earth up along either side of the leek row to give a longer section of white stem, but if plants were dropped into 6 ins deep holes this isn't really necessary. Because the plants are so hardy they can be left in the ground until needed, but any left by the beginning of March will need lifting and using, or they may start running up to seed.

Onions

Big bulb *onions* are not truly a salad crop, but medium-sized ones are fine for slicing thinly in salads, or can be chopped finely to blend with all kinds of other crunchy ingredients. There are a number of ways of growing onions, among them sowing seed in August to overwinter in the open, sowing seed in gentle heat in January to transplant to open ground in early spring, and sowing direct into a well-prepared site in March. However, for most of us these days, growing from sets is the first choice and that is the only way I'm going to consider here. Sets should be bought from a reliable source and I find it worth paying more for those of a guaranteed quality. 'Sturon' and 'Stuttgarter Giant' are good varieties to plant in late March or early April on good fertile soil that has been dug and manured in autumn, then left rough for wintry weather to help it crumble down to a fine tilth. New in the past couple of seasons are Unwins 'First Early' sets for autumn planting to give a midsummer harvest of onions to use before Christmas, but I don't think they will be so important for salads as the sets we plant in spring to harvest in late summer and store right through the cold months.

Plant your onion sets 3-4 ins apart in rows 10-12 ins apart, using the older wider spacings only if you want very large bulbs that are not ideal for salad use. Through the growing season it's important to keep the onion bed weed free, to hoe through a few times and to water in dry spells. When tops begin to turn yellow and flop over lift the crop carefully with a fork and spread the bulbs out to ripen and dry off, preferably on a netting frame that allows a good air circulation.

After ten days or so of drying, sort the bulbs, putting aside for immediate use any damaged in any way. Rope the larger bulbs and store smaller ones, like shallots, in plastic net bags hung from the shed roof.

Among the onions listed in the seed catalogues you will see 'The Queen' and 'Paris Silverskin' recommended as varieties for pickling. Seed sown thickly in a broad drill in spring in similar soil to that used for onion sets and left unthinned

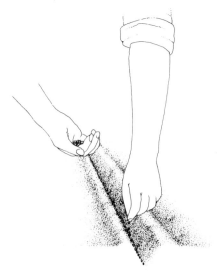

Figure 12: Sowing 'Paris Silverskin'-type pickling onions in broad drill, to give small bulbs to store for winter salads

through the growing season will produce a crop of small round white bulbs that come early and are superb for salad use if stored in net bags.

Chives

I could include *chives* with the other herbs, but as they belong to the *Allium* family I have put them in among the other onions. A must in any kitchen garden, they are splendid for salad use and I don't think I can imagine a garden without a row. For cold weather use the plants can be covered with cloches, or better still you can transplant some chives in late summer into the greenhouse border, into a no longer needed growing bag, or pot some up to grow on a windowsill indoors if you have no greenhouse.

Grow chives for use in the summer months in a row in the vegetable plot, in clumps in a herb bed, or as an edging to a flower bed, on ground that has been well enriched with

Figure 13: Chive clump being divided and replanted

humus. The grassy green foliage is attractive and you can allow the mauve thrift-like flowers to grow up if the herb is with your other decorative plants, though purists say flower buds should be nipped off before they waste the plant's energy that should all be going into food production. Wherever and however you grow this easy member of the onion family, you'll find it pays to cut the leaves regularly, even if not needed in the kitchen, as this encourages plenty of fresh tender 'grass'.

You'll find clumps increase quite quickly and are best lifted, divided and replanted in small sections every three years and when dividing you can use some of the tiny plantlets as substitute spring onions, but generally it is just the leaves that we use. Use these chopped as a garnish for your salads, or more liberally to blend into a mixed bowl for a stronger flavour of onion. Chives have the advantage that they can often be enjoyed by those who find onions indigestible.

There is a less common variety known as 'Giant Chives' which has thicker foliage, a slightly stronger flavour, and larger flowers that are more freely produced. Some say that this is too coarse for kitchen use, but others that it is an improvement on the small type. I think it is really a matter of personal preference and would certainly recommend trying the plant. If you find that you don't care for its leaves in salads, and I think that is unlikely, you will find it is excellent for edging borders.

Welsh Onion

The plant that is usually supplied if you go to a nursery for the *Welsh onion* should truly be called the ever-ready or everlasting onion, but I'm going to discuss this under the common false name. Like chives this is a clump-forming perennial with evergreen leaves and thickened white stems that look a bit like leek plants at the time we set them out in June and July. A most useful member of the onion family for winter salads, this is easy to grow and develops quite big clumps which are best lifted and divided every two or three years. You can either gather the leaves to chop in salads or, when clumps are large enough, lift out a few of the plants to use as a splendid substitute for spring onions at a time when they are not readily available. You will find these a bit stronger and a bit coarser than 'White Lisbon', but good value all the same.

The correct botanical name for the everlasting onion is

Allium cepa var. *perutile*, which tells us that it's simply one form of our big onion; in nursery lists, however, it may well be called *Allium fistulosum*, which is the name for the true Welsh onion. That dies back in winter to reappear once more in spring, flowers freely, and can be raised from seed sown in spring. You can use the plant for salads in summer, but it's not nearly so useful as the everlasting onion that's so often given its name, but doesn't flower and stays green through winter.

Tree Onion

Another less common member of the *Allium* family is the Egyptian or *tree onion* that sends up a stem of around 3 ft which ends not as you would expect in a flower, but is topped by a cluster of five or six shallot-like bulbs. Hardy and easy to grow, this likes good soil and is best sited in front of a trellis which allows you to tie in and support the top-heavy stems.

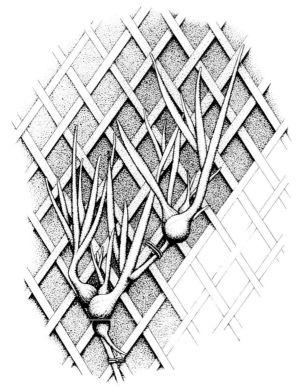

Figure 14: Tree onion growing against trellis. Stems are tied to trellis for support

Otherwise, they flop over, the new bulbs root before ripening, and you end up with a jungle of tree onions and weeds.

You can use the small bulbs in summer salads, or can allow them to ripen and then dry off and store like shallots. They are good for chopping or slicing to go in autumn mixed salads, or for serving whole with a few sticks of celery, a crisp dessert apple and a few slices of winter radish. Tree onions look ornamental at the back of a bed of those herbs, like mint and parsley, that do best on fertile land.

Garlic

The last member of the onion family that I think is important for salads is the *garlic*, and you can save quite a bit on housekeeping bills by growing this at home to give a store of cloves for winter use. Ideally given a light well-drained soil in a sunny open position, garlic likes fertile conditions, and does better on loose light soil than on clay.

Plant and grow this rather like the shallot, planting the bulb segments we call cloves 6 ins apart on well-cultivated land manured for the previous crop in late February and March. The pointed ends should be uppermost and only just covered by soil. Grow on until late summer, removing any flower buds that appear, and when the leaves start to die down lift carefully with a fork. Dry thoroughly in the sun and store in a cool frost-free place, setting aside a few bulbs for planting next season.

As each clove from the original bulb will produce a cluster of a dozen or more new cloves and a little goes a very long way, you can see that this is a value for money crop for small gardens. In fact, when space is very restricted you'll do far better to concentrate on more luxury crops like garlic than on everyday vegetables like big onions and cabbages.

Use garlic in salads with discretion. I believe the best way is to cut a clove and rub around the inside of the salad bowl before putting in the other ingredients, but some cooks like to use some raw very finely chopped garlic in their salad dressings.

Such an important vegetable family, the onions are a must for any salad lover. However limited the area of your garden, there must be space for a clump of the so-called Welsh onions, a pot or two of chives on a windowsill, or a short row of 'White Lisbon' spring onions in the border or, if that's not possible, in a growing bag once used for tomatoes.

CHAPTER 5

Cucumbers

Whether the mention of cucumber brings to mind elegant thin slices in tiny sandwiches at afternoon tea on the Vicarage lawn, or large chunks from a whole fruit shared between the family during a picnic meal in the country, you are sure to serve cucumber in your salads fairly often.

Proof of their popularity is shown by the latest statistics which tell us that over 100,000,000 are grown in this country a year, and that's not allowing for the many cucumbers produced by home gardeners, nor for the months when we rely on supplies from Holland, the Canary Islands and other countries overseas.

Now that so many more people own greenhouses, indoor cucumbers are a much more commonly grown crop for the home gardener, but even if you grow these do grow too the easy outdoor varieties with their tasty fruits grown in the open air. Don't think of them as seedy, yellowing, pimply affairs, for modern plant breeders have produced varieties that yield fruits perhaps equal in quality to any indoor cucumber. In fact, I've seen long smooth green outdoor fruits that only an expert could have been sure were not grown inside.

Of course, home production is out of the question for rather more than half the year and so then you'll have to rely on the shops. But, I never associate the cool succulent cucumber with winter eating and so it seldom goes in our cold weather salads. I much prefer to serve each foodstuff in its season and to change my ingredients around according to the weather and the month. Not for me Brussels sprouts and celery in June, nor cucumber and small red radishes in January.

Growing at home gives a choice of the unusual varieties and though today we have lost the bronze, yellow and blue varieties favoured by Victorians, we can try those types seldom, if ever, seen in the shops. In particular I'm thinking of the 'Crystal Apple' outdoor cucumber with round, pale, almost yellow, fruits that are very mild and more easily

Cucumbers

Figure 15: 'Crystal Apple' cucumber plant – with mature fruit and some blooms

digested than the usual kinds. Peeled thinly and cut into wedges, they can be eaten like a piece of fruit (which is why they are sometimes called apple cucumbers).

Historical Background

It's known that cucumbers were grown in India 3,000 years ago and in China 2,000 years before the birth of Christ, and were highly prized by the ancient Greeks. It's said that the first cucumbers were brought to Britain from the East Indies in 1573 and for 250 years after that they were considered a great delicacy by the wealthy. We may grumble at high prices in the months when the shops must rely on imported supplies or cucumbers raised in expensively-heated greenhouses, but early last century cow-cumbers, as they used to be called, could sell for as much as a guinea each and that was more than a workman's weekly wage. In fact, it was not until the outdoor ridge varieties became available that the cucumber became something for everyone to enjoy.

Cucumber is a source of vitamins B and C, but is not a particularly nutritious salad stuff. However, it is low in calories, and can therefore be eaten freely by slimmers.

Buying and Storing Cucumbers

If you rely on the shops, you can find cucumbers on sale all year round and in late summer the outdoor varieties will be available from some greengrocers as well as the usual greenhouse varieties. I never like those supermarket cucumbers that have been wrapped in a tight-fitting skin of plastic, as they never seem to keep for more than a day or two, but much prefer to buy unwrapped. When buying look for long straight fruits of a bright green that are evenly coloured with no hint of

40

the yellowing that could be a sign of age. For economy its worth buying cheap fruits that are crooked or mis-shapen, but avoid any that are swollen or have bulbous ends as they might be seedy and bitter.

The outdoor ridge cucumbers vary in quality a good deal, but you can't go wrong with those that are bright green, slim and fresh. Avoid any that are tubby or yellowed with ripening, as they are almost certain to contain big hard seeds.

Store cucumber in the salad drawer of the fridge, or if that's not possible store stem-end down, and cut end covered, in a glass of water away from strong light. Cucumber will keep for several days, but it's wiser to be generous the first couple of days, rather than to try and eke the fruit out all week and serve when past its best.

Serving Cucumber

I don't think I need to offer advice on how to serve this popular salad stuff, though I will say that I think it's near sacrilege to cook something that's so good to eat raw. For parties you can take a good straight greenhouse cucumber, cut it in halves lengthwise and scoop out the seeds to replace with a filling, perhaps of cottage cheese and chopped chives with a garnish of tiny tomato wedges; or can stuff $1\frac{1}{2}$-ins sections of a cucumber to up-end and make party snacks. But really all that fiddle is not necessary with something that's so good to eat with no preparation.

Growing Your Own Cucumbers

With heating costs so high I don't think it's worth attempting to plant out cucumbers in a home greenhouse before May. Those put out late in the month, when days should be getting up to summer heat, will usually come in nearly as soon as those put out early in May, with some heat given at night. You don't have to have a conventional glasshouse and I know one gardener who made a polythene tunnel from heavy quality plastic sheeting and some old gas piping. The first summer he put in three cucumbers down one side and was nearing his hundredth fruit when a late summer gale blew the structure down. By then though he had sold enough surplus cucumbers to neighbours to start a fund towards a better house next season.

Ridge cucumbers need no protection at all, though I much prefer to raise my plants in pots inside, because that gives an earlier start, especially if you also use cloches or some other protection in the first week or so outside. Grown from seed

41

sown *in situ* in the open garden, they are at such risk to late frost and the slugs that so love tender young cucumber seed leaves.

Indoor

It takes about a month to raise a cucumber plant for putting out in the greenhouse or garden and so mid-April is plenty soon enough to start those for a cold house and later in the month those for the open ground. I sow seeds in individual 3-ins pots of John Innes seed compost, stand these in soft margarine tubs so that they can be watered from the bottom and cover with plastic domes, which I often economise on by making from plastic soft drink bottles cut into two. Sow the seeds on edge and place the pots in a warm room to ensure speedy germination. An alternative is to use an electric propagator either at one end of the greenhouse or indoors.

In the greenhouse you can plant out direct into the border after working plenty of well-rotted manure or garden compost into the soil; you can move the plants on to big 10-ins chrysanthemum pots for the rest of their life; or you can plant in growing bags, with two plants to a bag. In the border, allow at least 2 ft between plants. They used to say that you couldn't

Figure 16: Sowing cucumber seed on edge in pot of John Innes seed compost

grow tomatoes and cucumbers together in the same house, which was an awful nuisance because most of us want to grow both and few have two greenhouses. Now the problem has been solved, as it's so easy to partition off one end of the house with plastic sheeting to give a warmer humid place for cucumbers.

Greenhouse cucumbers are produced without pollination and it was important to pick all the male flowers off the old varieties, because fertilised blooms led to poorly-shaped fruits that were often bitter and seedy. Now we have varieties that have only female flowers, or so few males that it's very little bother to pick them off. Seeds cost more, but they are worth that, for the busy person at business all week just couldn't cope with de-blossoming. Buy a packet of the F1 hybrids like 'Femspot' or 'Pepinex 69' and you'll only have half a dozen seeds, but that's probably enough to share with a friend as each plant crops so abundantly.

If you use large pots for cropping cucumbers, I'd suggest the John Innes potting compost No. 3, which is the basic mixture plus 12 ozs of base fertiliser per bushel. Throughout the growing season, very regular watering will be necessary – the soil should never dry out, but should never be waterlogged either, and you'll need also to liquid feed regularly.

Plants can be trained up bamboo canes to the house roof and then will need stopping to encourage lateral growths, which should each be pinched out at two leaves. The canes won't be enough to support all the crop and so you can supplement with horizontal wires spaced about 1 ft apart, or can use plastic string netting. Supporting strings or wires need to be about 1 ft from the glass so the plants grow behind the support and the fruits hang down between.

Usually the plants will regulate their crops by dropping tiny fruits when too many have set, but if you do find too many its better to nick some out with a sharp knife, or you may end up with a lot of small cucumbers instead of large top quality specimens.

Outdoor

Ridge cucumbers in the open or partly under cloches are a crop that I've always found very easy and very rewarding. They need little room and you can economise on space by training the trailing stems up a trellis, specially if you go for the Japanese climbing varieties that are best grown up a trellis or tripod of canes. Some of their fruits grow to about 2 ft long and are far more likely to be of long, smooth greenhouse quality if hanging from a frame than if grown on the flat where the developing cucumbers may run into plant stems, be diverted and end up looking like boomerangs.

My ridge cucumber seeds sown late in April in pots in the warmth of the house are moved out to the cold greenhouse once well up and in milder seasons I have very successfully sown in pots in the greenhouse. They cannot safely go out completely into the open until frost risk is past, but planting in the third week in May is safe if you cover with cloches or individual plastic dome pot covers for a couple of weeks. Pinch growing tips out of ridge cucumbers at the fifth leaf to encourage sideshoots and after that let them develop as they like.

Choose a sunny open position and, for the climbing varieties, one that's sheltered from strong wind. They all need a fertile soil that's moisture retentive and I like to dig lots of well-rotted manure or compost into the site.

If you do that, you should end with a slight ridge, but I find plants do just as well on the flat so long as water cannot collect around the base of the main stem. Put out at just the right stage with one pair of true leaves, pot-grown cucumbers will suffer no root disturbance and no check to growth. If you have not raised your own and need to buy plants, look for those with a few fresh green leaves and avoid taller yellowing plants that will almost certainly have been growing too long and be pot-bound.

Figure 17: Pinching out growing tip of ridge cucumber at fifth true leaf stage

Through the growing season you'll need to water outdoor cucumbers in dry weather and will find it pays to dose regularly with Phostrogen or one of the other proprietary feeds. A mulch of lawn mowings or peat will help keep roots cool, prevent weeds developing and stop the earth making cucumbers muddy.

You won't need to pick male flowers off ridge cucumbers as it doesn't matter if they are pollinated, but I'm most impressed by the new 'Amslic' F_1 hybrid that doesn't produce male blooms. Another excellent variety among the modern kinds is 'Burpee Hybrid', while you'll do well with 'Perfection King of the Ridge'. During the cropping season you'll need to look over the cucumber patch nearly ever day, for fruits develop very quickly and won't keep coming if you've allowed some early ones to ripen and form seeds.

If you've no greenhouse and no space in the garden, you can still grow outdoor varieties, by planting in growing bags or boxes filled with a mixture of John Innes potting compost No. 3 and well-rotted manure. Stand these on a balcony or in a sunny back yard, train the trailing stems up a small trellis or tripod of canes and you'll have decorative and productive plants to allow you to be more generous with cucumber in the summer months.

CHAPTER 6

Beetroot

No one would describe pale boiled beetroot that's been smothered in vinegar as an exciting salad. But, I think a beetroot wrapped in aluminium foil and baked in the oven so none of the colour and goodness can escape is delectable when sliced and simply dressed with olive oil and a sprinkling of finely chopped chives or parsley.

In fact, I think a great many beetroots are well grown by gardeners and then ruined by cooks like the woman I used to know who would put the round red roots in a large saucepan and then cover them in water before boiling. Needless to say they cooked to a poor colour and white rings showed so much that her husband thought he must be growing a poor variety!

Historical Background

Beetroot have been cultivated for at least a thousand years and were among the foods offered to Apollo, the Greek god, at Delphos by the ancients. No one seems sure when they were introduced to Britain, but the sixteenth-century herbalist John Gerard recommended beetroot served with oil, vinegar and salt as a winter salad. In her famous Victorian *Book of Household Management*, Mrs Beeton said that the beetroot made an excellent addition to winter salads and that the vegetable was exceedingly wholesome and nutritious. Modern authorities report no specially high food value in the root, but it does contain modest amounts of a number of substances necessary in a well-balanced diet.

Buying Beetroot

In the shops you can buy beetroot ready-cooked and this will usually be sliced and covered with transparent film at the supermarket and still whole in the skins at the greengrocers. That costs more, and saves time, but I prefer to buy raw and do my own cooking. Sometimes you may have difficulty in tracking down a shop that sells raw roots, but they can be found in the greengrocers that cater for discerning shoppers and are available through many months of the year. In early summer there will be rather pricey bunches of delicious young beetroot with fresh leaves proclaiming that it's not long since they were pulled. Later there will be globe beet sold in bunches or by weight with the tops twisted off. Look for firm fresh roots without broken skin or other damage and aim for tennis ball size, as small roots without tops are usually of inferior quality and large ones can prove coarse and show white rings when cooked. From Christmas to spring the best buy are the long roots of the 'Cheltenham Green Top'-type that store better than globe beetroot and cook very well, each root giving many slices.

Don't buy many beetroot at one time, for summer roots are much best eaten fresh and though winter ones store well in damp sand or peat they tend to shrivel fairly soon after being taken from store and moved to a warmer atmosphere. When preparing them to cook, twist off the tops, as cutting the leaves and stems away can encourage bleeding and loss of colour. Wash well to remove all traces of garden dirt, but

Cooking Beetroot

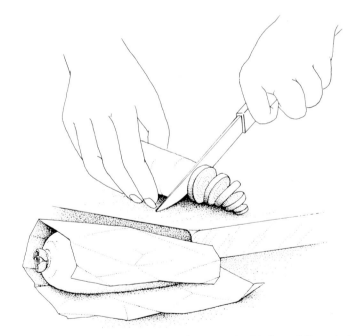

Figure 18: Wrapping cylindrical beetroot in kitchen foil to bake. Cooked beet being sliced

don't use a scrubbing brush or you will risk damage to the skins.

You may feel it extravagant to put the oven on just for beetroot, but you can bake two or three roots whilst you are cooking something else in the oven, say a batch of cakes, or some jacket potatoes. Those tender little summer beet of golf ball size can be cooked in the same way, but then I wrap four or five in a parcel of foil instead of wrapping individually. Alternatively, I sometimes bake them in a casserole containing just enough water to prevent their catching but not enough to leave any liquid at the end of cooking time – the younger and more tender they are the less cooking time is needed. You can tell when a beetroot is done because then the skin will rub off easily when pushed with the fingers. Prodding with a fork to test for softness can cause bleeding.

Serving
Beetroot

Some cooks use quite a lot of cooked ingredients in salads, but I don't agree with them. To me, a dish that includes cooked cold potatoes, beans, cauliflower or carrots is simply cold vegetables and a real salad should be made up of raw foodstuffs. I do make an exception, however, for beetroot, because although you can serve small amounts finely grated I don't care for the flavour. I don't often mix beetroot in with other salad stuffs, as the red will so quickly run and spoil the look of paler ingredients, though sometimes I'll dice beet and mix with yoghurt, cottage cheese or soured cream; or with diced cold cooked potatoes and mayonnaise to give a deliberately pink centre to a salad platter.

More often I'll serve beetroot as a side dish to accompany a mixed salad; or with celery, tomatoes, lettuce and other salad stuffs all served separately. I must add that I never use cochineal or other red colouring with my beetroot, but relying on cooking so their natural red is retained.

Growing Your
Own Beetroot

In the home garden you've the choice of all the varieties in the seed lists and can grow the round, long and cylindrical types. The latter are seldom seen in the shops, but are becoming increasingly popular as each long oval root will give far more slices than a round beet of the same diameter, but needs no more space in the garden to develop. You can also enjoy your beet straight from the row and I think every gardener will agree that roots bought from a shop never taste as good as tender young ones pulled just before cooking.

You may not feel beetroot should be a top choice for growing in a greenhouse, but an early row in the border of a cold structure will give tasty young roots at that time in early summer when shop prices are high and a variety of fresh salad stuffs is still hard to find. One friend of mine always grows a row in his cold house from a late February/early March sowing and is pulling delicious bunches while plants in the open in his neighbours' gardens are still small.

They used to advise against sowing the seed before April, as older varieties had a nasty habit of running up to seed instead of developing roots if put in too soon. Modern breeding, though, has given us varieties like the 'Avon Early' raised from the 'Detroit Globe' beetroot at the National Vegetable Research Station at Wellesbourne especially for early production, though good too for succession. You can safely sow this or the similar 'Boltardy' in the open in March, or a little earlier in a cold greenhouse or under cloches. Use these to start a couple of rows and then move onto some dwarf tomatoes or other half-hardy salad crop in May.

Beetroot grow best on land manured for the previous crop, and I prefer to sow my early rows on ground dug in autumn and left in rough clods for the winter weather to help the soil crumble down into a fine tilth. For the first sowing I like to choose a sunny part of the garden where drainage is good, but for later sowings my heavy clay has proved very productive.

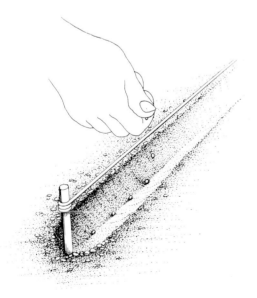

Figure 19: Sowing beet seed 1 in apart in inch-deep drill

Position cloches a fortnight before you intend to sow, as this will warm and dry the soil. Otherwise, wait for a drying March wind to make the soil easy to work, then rake in a dressing of 2 ozs per sq yd of general fertiliser before making 1 in deep drills 10-12 ins apart.

What looks like one beetroot seed is strictly speaking a cluster of seeds, and that is why seedlings tend to come up in groups and have to be thinned. Sow carefully with the seed clusters a good inch apart for round varieties and 2 ins apart for the long type, then take out alternate plants as soon as they are large enough to handle. Thin the long type again by removing alternate plants at around 6 ins high and the globe type by pulling alternate roots for early eating at golf ball size, leaving the others to fill out to the ideal tennis ball size.

You can be thrifty and use the first thinnings to make another row, for tiny beet seedlings transplant well and will make roots of equal quality to those grown on *in situ*.

Birds adore the young red leaves of beetroot, and I find it essential to cover my seed drills with plastic fruit netting or the seedlings will be devoured almost before they are through the ground. Slugs are very keen on chewing into the roots at that time when they are just beginning to be fit to pull, so it's

Figure 20: Wringing off tops from beet ready for storing

important, especially in a wet summer, to put down slugkiller – well-protected so it's not eaten by birds or household pets.

Sow 'Avon Early' under cloches or in a cold house at the end of winter and use this, or another of the Detroit globe type, in succession for monthly sowings until June. Or change in April to the long oval varieties that go so much farther, choosing 'Cylindra' or the newer 'Formanova'. In May put in 'Cheltenham Green Top', 'Long Blood Red' or 'Covent Garden' to give long maincrop roots to lift in October, then wring off their tops and store in boxes of sand or peat in a cool, frost-free shed for winter eating. Lastly, sow a row of the globe 'Little Ball', or of 'Cylindra', in early July to give fresh young roots for autumn salads.

If you like to try uncommon crops, do try 'Burpee's Golden Beet' with yellow-fleshed roots and tops that can be cooked to eat like spinach, thus making it a useful dual-purpose variety for the small garden. Like me, you may feel that beetroot should be red, but the golden roots have the big advantage that they don't lose colour in cooking and can safely be mixed with other salad stuffs without spoiling their colours. Diced they look good with white chopped celery, green shredded Brussels sprouts and red tomato. The flavour is reckoned to be very good.

Even more unusual is the globe beetroot 'Albina Vereduna' (you may find this listed as 'Snowhite'), that some believe tastes better than the red. Of course, this can safely be mixed with other salad ingredients with no fear of marring their colours and the ice-white slices can look good with green lettuce and cucumber and red tomato and pepper. It's something to show off as a novelty when you have friends in for a meal, for all gardeners like to grow something that's different.

If your garden is too small to allow room for a full succession of different beetroots for eating from midsummer through to next spring, I'd advise concentrating on the early rows and July sowings to give the nicest young beet for pulling young and fresh. Buying from the shops won't be too costly or too difficult in August and September when fresh supplies are plentiful and through winter you can rely on them for stored roots. I must add that you'll certainly have to grow your own if you want to serve the golden and white beet, and you are not so likely to find the cylindrical type in the shops.

Whether you grow your own or buy, do cook well to preserve the colour and goodness and do try some more exciting

Beetroot

dressing than vinegar. I don't think you can better olive oil and a garnish of chopped chives, parsley or tarragon; and think cottage cheese and beetroot is an ideal marriage.

CHAPTER 7

Carrots

Some people would think of the carrot mainly as a vegetable to cook and serve hot, but it is one of my main choices for salads almost all through the year. Although in summer I do very occasionally use leftover cooked young roots in a mixed salad, this isn't a way I would recommend. I think that young or old carrots are delicious raw, and served in this way they can have lost none of their goodness in cooking and will help maintain healthy teeth.

With many vegetables the nutrient level is lower after they have been stored, but carrots are every bit as nourishing after being kept for several months in sand or peat in a shed as when fresh pulled from the garden in summer. Carrots provide 14 per cent of our vitamin A intake, so vital for growth, bone and tooth development, healthy skin and eyes, night vision and prevention of infection; by being generous in your use of carrots you are contributing considerably to the well-being of your family. The roots also contain vitamin C and some of the minerals the body needs. For growing children a raw carrot munched mid-morning or at the end of a meal is a much better snack than crisps and sweets.

Historical Background

The varieties of carrot we know today have been developed over centuries from the wild carrot that can be found in many parts of Europe in fields, by the wayside and by the seashore. There is one account of the plant being sown in a monastery garden in 1419, but carrots do not seem to have been widely grown or appreciated as part of our diet until the arrival of the Huguenot refugees in the sixteenth century.

Buying and Serving Carrots

If you have to buy from the shops supplies are good in most months, only becoming intermittent and of dubious quality in early spring. Even then you can often find good roots, though it is important not to buy too many at a time and to look for well-coloured carrots that are firm and juicy in appearance. Among imported supplies obtainable when our own have finished the new crop from Cyprus is among the best, though these roots do tend to be drier.

The time when you have to watch British carrots most is after a spell of very hard weather, for frost can make them mushy and of poor flavour. From the middle of spring you will see bunches of new season's roots sold with the tops on and though costly these are delicious when really fresh, but soon wither and deteriorate. The freshness of the foliage will indicate how long since they left the ground.

From the midsummer to March the best buy will be maincrop stump-rooted samples free of any sign of damage from pests or mechanical lifting. Again, watch for firm, well-coloured roots of a convenient size and shape for grating. Once home with your carrots wash, and store in the salad drawer of the fridge. When preparing for table cut off top and bottom and scrape, or peel very thinly.

Few of us are able to grow enough carrots to provide our own supply through many months, but even a tiny garden should allow space for an early row to give those delicious finger-sized summer roots that are much tastier if used soon after pulling. Try also to grow a row from a midsummer sowing to give fresh young roots in autumn when shop supplies are almost always of large maincrop roots.

Serve those first young carrots, thinnings from the main-crop, and small roots from a late sowing, whole, sliced or quartered lengthwise in your salads. The larger maincrop roots can be sliced thinly, cut into match-sized strips, or coarsely grated; but I believe it is far better to use a fine grater for this makes the carrot far easier and pleasanter to eat. Finely grated carrot can be mixed with many other salad ingredients, but is specially good with crunchy shredded cabbage, chopped celery and diced dessert apple in autumn and winter; and with lettuce and chopped salad onions in summer.

Growing Your Own Carrots

The most important carrots from the garden are those that come earliest in the season and so they are one of my priorities for protection of some kind. You can sow in the open in March if weather permits, but seed can go in the border of a cold greenhouse, in a frame or under cloches positioned a fortnight earlier to warm and dry the soil, in February to start pulling in mid-May. For this early work I use 'Amsterdam

Forcing' with medium length, blunt-ended roots of superb quality.

The early sowing under cover avoids the carrot root fly that can be such a troublesome pest with later outdoor rows. I strongly object to chemical pesticides and use very few in my garden, but I do make an exception for carrots grown in the open, as otherwise root fly can ruin the entire crop. Cultural control measures will depend on the early covered sowings and rows put in after the first week in June, as both of these miss the first batch of the fly. It also helps to sow thinly, to thin or pull in the evening or on damp dull days, as the female fly is attracted to lay her eggs in bright sunny weather; and it is important to remove any foliage or thinnings immediately and to water the row before or just after pulling. It helps if the crop is moved around the plot, so that carrots are not sown on the same land more than once in three or four years, and a lot of people believe that growing onions alongside the carrots helps mask the smell that so attracts the fly. That being said, I must admit that I use Bromophos sprinkled in the seed drill and dusted along the row after thinning – never pull for table roots from a row dusted less than ten days before.

Figure 21: Raking general fertiliser into soil worked down to a fine tilth, for sowing carrots

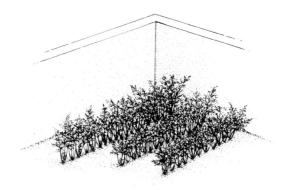

Figure 22: Bed of carrots with short rows 2-3 ins apart – for early bunching – in greenhouse border or cold frame

Carrots like good drainage and a sunny open site. When possible grow them on land manured for last season's vegetables, then deeply and thoroughly dug in autumn or early winter. Once March winds have dried out the rough clods you left when digging, it should not be too hard work to rake down the soil into a fine tilth for sowing. While doing this, work in a dressing of 2-3 ozs per sq yd of general fertiliser.

The traditional method was to sow in ¹₂-in deep drills 1 ft apart, but now we know that rows at 6 ins apart will give a higher yield of good medium-sized roots from a given area. It has also been discovered that growing in a bed with say ten short rows sown very thinly and spaced only 2-3 ins apart is extremely good utilisation of land and splendid for growing early bunching carrots. One friend of mine tried the method last year and reckoned that he had his best crop ever, with lots of finger-sized roots that he put down in his deep freeze for winter cooking. For the maincrop I think you'll do better to stick to rows with say five at 6 ins apart and then a wider space to allow access to the bed.

Delay sowing your maincrop until a week into June to avoid those early root flies and there is ample time to grow plump roots of an ideal size for the kitchen. When you want carrots for grating you don't want long tapering roots of the intermediate type, but a stump-rooted maincrop with richly-coloured flesh of fine texture and small core like 'Chantenay Red Cored'.

Alternatively, you can use the cylindrical stump-ended

'Nantes-Tip Top' that grows to about 6 ins long, has a sweet flavour and coreless very brightly-coloured flesh. Use this also for successional sowings in the open from March to mid-summer, for it's a variety good both for early pulling and storing.

If you are unlucky enough to have very shallow soil, I'd recommend the early maincrop 'Kundulus', with almost globe-shaped roots about 1¹₂ ins across and almost twice this length. Obviously weight of crop won't equal that when 6-ins roots of the same diameter are grown, but with this type soil depth is not important.

The row from a late June or July sowing, on land cleared from first peas, potatoes or other summer crop, will give tasty new carrots for October/November pulling and can safely be left in the ground until the beginning of December unless winter comes very early.

The top priority with this, as with all other midsummer vegetable sowings, is to ensure speedy germination and growth while the warmest weather is with us. That means making sure that the ground is moist enough for quick development and will almost certainly mean watering! Before forking or rotovating over the ground I find it is often best to soak overnight, particularly as this can make the work much easier. You can assist germination by soaking the bottom of the seed drills, or in very dry weather by making them twice as deep as normal and then lining with damp peat to retain moisture. Watering the row or patch in dry spells for the rest of summer will make the difference between a good crop and a bad one.

That may sound like a lot of work but, as I said earlier, this late carrot sowing is one of the most important, for those tender new carrots in autumn can bring a reminder of the summer that has gone and give variety that the salad bowl needs then. Give the sowing a priority, but even more important do try and make way for a patch of carrots sown in late winter under cold glass or plastic to come in with the swallows in late spring.

Storing Carrots

At the end of October lift your maincrop carrots, cut or twist off the tops, rub off surplus soil and put out any with the least hint of pest damage, splitting or scars of any kind, for early use. Store sound roots in boxes of dry sand or peat in a cool frost-free shed until required in the kitchen. You can leave carrots in the ground until needed if tops are cut down to 2 ins and a blanket of straw is placed over the bed for frost protection. But, beware, as this will allow any odd root fly maggots to feast away and slugs will also enjoy a nibble at the sweet orange-scarlet roots.

Figure 23: Packing maincrop stump-rooted carrots in boxes of peat, for storing in shed

Don't look upon carrots as a substitute salad ingredient for the times when tomatoes, lettuce and cucumber are in short supply, but as a mainstay of the salad bowl at all seasons and one that is very nourishing and far more sustaining than the green leaf salad stuffs. That makes finely grated carrot a must for those slimmers who want to cut out bread, potatoes and other starchy foods.

CHAPTER 8

Celery and Celeriac

These days you can buy celery at almost any time of year – but I never add any to summer salads. For, to me, celery is one of those nice things to look forward to as the days shorten and the leaves turn to flame and crimson. It's then that I start to think of crunchy salads with celery, grated carrot and shredded cabbage as the main ingredients instead of the lettuce, tomatoes and cucumbers we've been enjoying so much through the warm weeks of late summer.

Both celery and celeriac have been developed from the same wild plant that's a native of Britain, and was once cultivated under the name smallage for medicinal purposes. Some plant breeders aimed for better stalks and leaves and gradually developed celery as we know it today, while others worked on the roots and eventually produced the swollen stem bases that became known as turnip-rooted celery, or celeriac. Known in Tudor and Stuart times, celery was not commonly grown here until the eighteenth century after plants had been much improved. In a book published in the middle of the last century, celeriac is mentioned as easier and cheaper to grow, but even now is not grown on a large scale in this country. Celery is rich in valuable minerals, contains vitamins C and vitamins of the B complex and plenty of fibre to aid digestion. Like many other vegetables it is much more nutritious when eaten raw than when cooked.

Historical Background

In the shops there are two kinds of celery. The one you see most often and can buy in so many months is the self-blanching type that's grown on the flat, is washed and clean and may have been grown in Britain or imported from Israel or America. Not seen nearly so much now as a few years back is the blanched celery grown in a trench and sold with some of

Buying Celery

59

the dark soil from the fenland, where it grows so well, adhering to the white sticks.

I'm one of those people who think this has the real celery flavour and would always prefer to buy a head wrapped in newspaper to protect my other shopping from garden dirt than a clinically clean pre-packed head. Whichever you go for, do choose a head that's thick at the base, has smooth thick stalks and pale green leaves – if all the leaf has been cut off that could be a sign that foliage was withered and the head stale.

Once home, wash celery to use right away or store in a plastic box in the fridge. If the head looks limp, trim a bit away from the root and stand neck deep in cold water for a few hours to restore crispness.

There's no need to make any suggestions for using celery, for everyone knows that sticks served alone in an upright glass or laid out on a dish are very good. Do also try chopped celery in mixed salads, for that makes use of the slightly tougher outer stalks and helps create some superb blends of ingredients.

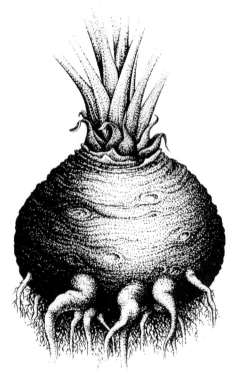

Figure 24: Close up of celeriac root

Celery and Celeriac

Not nearly so well known as celery is its near relative the celeriac – a knobbly, brown, turnip-like root you can find in specialist greengrocers in autumn and winter. With most vegetables there's a lot of goodness just under the skin and so it's best to eat the peel or pare it very thinly, but with this you have to cut thickly to peel off the bumpy surface. I wouldn't attempt to eat the outer part of the root raw, but after peeling take off another layer to go in the soup that celeriac makes so well, or use this as a cooked vegetable, leaving the best central part to slice thinly, grate, dice or cut into thin strips for salads. As one root may be the size of a good swede, there's plenty of flesh to use in several ways.

Buying Celeriac

Celery is not one of the easiest salad crops to grow well, especially if you aim for the traditional type that is normally grown in a trench and earthed up to give tender blanched stalks, but it's a challenge that any keen gardener likes to take on and there's immense satisfaction in serving a well-grown head that you have cared for from seed to table. Very much easier is the modern type that is grown on the flat and needs little or no blanching to prepare the heads for table. Celeriac is also grown on the flat and as the roots, like most unusual vegetables, are costly to buy, it certainly pays to grow at home.

Growing Your Own Celery

Both celery and celeriac need starting off under glass to give plants to go outside when frost risk is past. You can buy in boxes of plants in May or June, but that gives a limited choice of variety and is not necessary, as seedlings are easy to raise at home even if you've no heat. My greenhouse is cold and so I don't rely on that for germination. Instead, I sow seed in 3-ins pots of John Innes seed compost in March, stand them in my favourite soft margarine tub for saucers to allow watering from the base, and cover with plastic dome tops. My improvised propagating frames are stood on a warm windowsill, with the compost kept moist until seedlings appear after 2-3 weeks. Germination rate is high and so seed is sown thinly, and because it will stay viable for at least two years I always make a packet last for two seasons.

Once seedlings are well up I move the pots, now uncovered, to a cooler part of the house and then to the cold greenhouse to be pricked out, as soon as true leaves begin to show, into seed trays of John Innes potting compost No. 1, with $1\frac{1}{2}$-2ins each way between the baby plants. If you are growing celery and celeriac, or more than one type of celery, do take care to

Celery and Celeriac

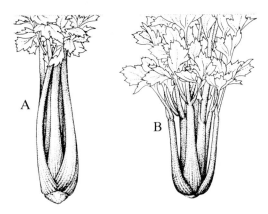

Figure 25: Two types of celery head: (A) trenched 'Giant Red', (B) 'Golden self-blanching'

label from seed sowing to planting outside, for I defy anyone to be sure they can tell the seedlings apart and nothing would be more frustrating than to plant the type that grows on the flat in a trench and vice versa.

If you can manage to grow more than one type I'd advise doing so, for they have different uses. The varieties that are grown on the flat without blanching come in early, the 'Golden Self-blanching' usually being ready at the end of August, but are not frost hardy and so cannot be relied on late in the season. Of the traditional blanched type the white has by far the best flavour and is excellent for eating from October to Christmas, while the pink will go on a bit longer, and the red though of not such a good flavour can be relied on to go into New Year. Celeriac can be used in autumn, but I tend to hold mine back until most of the celery has been eaten, for this will generally go on through winter.

From this you'll see that a small number of several kinds will be of far more value for the salad bowl than one big planting. If space is very limiting I'd opt for the 'American Green' that needs no blanching, comes in around October when summer salad stuffs are coming to an end, and frost permitting can go on into January. I once lost my crop in a sudden severe spell at the beginning of December, but that could have been avoided if I had had sense enough to throw some straw over the bed when hard frost was forecast. Some say the flavour compares poorly with blanched celery, but my family think it's delicious.

All the members of the celery family like rich well-drained ground best, though the types grown on the flat don't mind heavy land so much. If you are on heavy clay making a trench is no joke and you'll find that a damp trench on this type of land attracts slugs, and that once they have chewed holes in the hearts of your heads, rot can set in and ruin the crop.

On the Flat

Prepare the site for celery on the flat in winter or early spring by digging in well-rotted manure or garden compost at the rate of a bucketful to every square yard. In May put out the hardened off plants at 9 ins each way using a trowel to lift them from the seed tray, which should have been thoroughly soaked with water the night before so soil adheres to the roots. Handle carefully and roots need not be much disturbed. Plant firmly and water in well. Don't grow this kind of celery in a row, but in a block as this helps the plants blanch one another. A block 5 ft × 5 ft feet will take 50 plants and to make sure the ones on the outside are blanched it is wise to surround the block with wooden boards held up on edge by short stakes, or by tucking straw in among the row around the outside of the block.

The wild celery is a plant of the waterside and boggy land and all its garden forms need lots of moisture in the growing season to give the best results. Fertile land well supplied with organic matter helps, but I find it vitally important to water well and regularly in most years, not giving small cans, but really soaking the ground every 10-14 days. Unless your land is in exceptionally good heart, I'd also advise a few doses of Phostrogen or one of the other liquid feeds to boost growth, always applying the feed to damp soil.

In a Trench

Prepare a trench for the traditional type of celery in winter by taking out soil to a depth of 1 ft and a width of 15 ins. Fork a bucketful of well-rotted manure or garden compost into the bottom of every 6 ft run of the trench and then replace soil to within 3 ins of ground level. As planting out doesn't take place until late May or early June, there's time to grow a quick catch crop of radishes or early lettuce before the celery goes in.

Just before planting rake an oz of general fertiliser into

every yard run of the trench bottom, then set out the plants at 9 ins apart in a double staggered row. As with celery on the flat, watering in well and very regular watering through the growing season is essential. When plants are well grown and about 1 ft high, usually in August, tie the stalks together loosely, remove outer yellowed leaves and any sideshoots that are developing and prepare to start blanching. You can do this by earthing up with soil to just below the leaves, repeating the operation every three weeks until the trench is filled in and earth is piled up on either side of the row of plants to give sloping sides.

I remember one old countryman telling me that they grew celery so well in the garden of the Kentish stately home where he had worked that in autumn a tall man could stand between the earthed up rows and be completely hidden from sight. I don't imagine you'll want to blanch nearly such a long length of stem, but the longer the better for eating.

To give the best clean heads for exhibition showmen wrap their celery in collars made from corrugated or brown paper or from black polythene, before earthing up, and I believe that's an excellent idea in the garden to produce the top table quality. Whether you do this or rely on earthing alone do take care not to drop soil down among the leaf stalks during the operation and tackle the job when leaves and stalks are dry but soil is moist, for soil earthed up when dry will remain that way and hinder growth.

Figure 26: Cut-away to show wrapping of celery in corrugated paper collars before earthing up

I've already said that slugs are a great pest of the crop. I find it important to put down slug bait near the row, taking care that this is covered so that it cannot be reached by the family pets and wild birds.

Most people agree that the flavour of celery is better after a sharp frost and so I would not start to dig from my trench until the garden had been coated with white on a few mornings. Try to grow several varieties of this valuable cold weather salad to give the longest possible home-grown season and never worry about producing too much, for what isn't needed in the salad bowl can be cooked as a main vegetable or used in soups and stews.

Growing Your Own Celeriac

Celeriac, like self-blanching celery, is grown on the flat and doesn't involve a great deal of work. Seedlings are raised in the same way from a March sowing to go outside in early June and again need a site well fed with rotted manure during winter. Before planting, rake in about 3 ozs per sq yd of general fertiliser and then set out the young celeriac at 1 ft apart each way, firming in and watering well, and with a dusting of Bromophos to ward off the carrot fly that can seriously damage the roots.

Through summer, water very generously in dry spells and dose with liquid feed every fortnight. Remove old leaves as they die and any sideshoots that appear, as this helps encourage the stem bases to swell into the turnip-like root we want for table.

The crop is usually ready in October and can be left in the ground until needed, unless you are in a cold area, providing you throw some straw or bracken over the bed when very hard frost is forecast. Alternatively, you can lift the plants, trim off leaves and store in boxes of sand or peat in a dry, frost-free place: but celeriac is so much nicest used soon after lifting that I'd be loath to do that. 'Globus' is a good variety that's been around for some years, while the newer 'Jose' makes large roots and because it produces little foliage can be planted a wee bit closer together.

When you buy celeriac all the leaves will have been trimmed off, but when you bring in from the garden don't waste the tops. The best outer stalks and leaves can go in the soup pan and all the centre stalks and leaves are fine for chopping in mixed salads.

When you lift trenched celery or celeriac from the garden

you'll find much the easiest way to clean is with the garden hose with your thumb pressed halfway across the end to increase water pressure. This soon removes all traces of earth with no risk of bruising and scratching as you can so easily do when a scrubbing brush is used. This also avoids a mess in the kitchen sink!

If your family like salads you are certain to use celery and I believe it's very important to grow at least some of your own supply at home, for only then can you enjoy the freshest plants and the most delicious flavour.

CHAPTER 9

Chicory

There have been some exciting developments among salad stuffs in recent years and one that has made a big difference to the choice during the cold months is the introduction to this country of chicory that can be grown completely in the open. Now we have several varieties to sow in our gardens to give material for salads in the weeks of autumn and winter when lettuce is almost impossible to produce at home.

Those white chicons you see in the shops are produced from the old-style 'Witloof' variety of chicory that needs lifting and forcing indoors before giving any salad material. You can grow these at home, but it is rather a bother and so few gardeners make the effort. However, anyone with a few square yards of fertile soil can produce a good crop of the easy chicory of the 'Sugar Loaf'-type that blanches itself in the row.

A relation of the dandelion, the large-rooted chicory earned the name 'Witloof' (Flemish for white leaf) from the practice of blanching its leaves. It's said that the method originated when a Belgian farmer threw some old roots that he had used to make coffee into a dark shed and discovered by accident that they sent up tender white shoots that were good to eat. From that sprang up the commercial production of the chicons we buy in the shops. The 'Sugar Loaf' chicory is an old variety that originated in the Lombardy and Piedmont regions of Italy, loaf being one of the words used in those parts to describe a chicory head. The outer leaves protect the heart so tightly that leaves are self-blanched and far sweeter than those of many of the other chicories grown and eaten in Italy.

Now, I see, that the seedsmen are offering the red-leaved 'Verona' chicory that needs cold weather to turn from green and develops tight solid heads to protect itself from wintry weather. This can be forced either by lifting and treating like 'Witloof', or by covering with straw or earth in the open, but

Historical Background

67

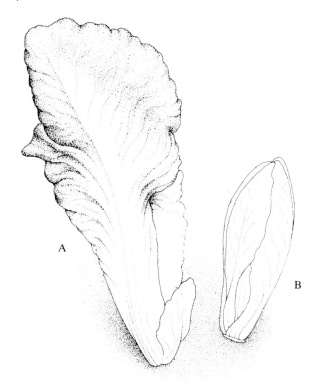

Figure 27: (A) Head of 'Sugar Loaf'-type chicory, (B) forced chicon of 'Witloof' type

that is not necessary for heads are good to eat when grown naturally and because they are hardier than the 'Sugar Loaf'-type will last into New Year.

Buying and Serving Chicory

If you go to the shops you will probably find only the forced chicons with conical heads of crisp white leaves about 6 ins long. Buy only those that look young and firm with no hint of withered leaves, and once home wash to use right away or store in the salad drawer of the fridge until needed.

It's possible you will see the larger pale creamy-green heads of the 'Sugar Loaf'-type chicory in a specialist greengrocer's shop or one of those small market stalls that buys from home growers. Look for fresh leaves and a firm chicon, as that will have the best heart – heads are very much larger than forced chicons and look rather more like Chinese cabbage. Each one will go a long way and so it's wise to buy only when you are planning several salad meals in the next few days.

I wouldn't serve either type of chicory alone in the way we serve lettuce, but find their pale crisp leaves are ideal for shredding to make the base of a cold weather salad, or mixed in with a variety of other ingredients. Some people complain that the leaves are slightly bitter and I have come across those who sprinkle them with caster sugar. I'd rather counteract the slight bitterness with something sweet: a diced dessert apple, some grapes, chopped dates, seedless raisins or sultanas. Alternatively, you can serve beetroot as a side dish. Chicory blends particularly well with citrus fruit and the segments of a sweet orange also go with it especially well, or if, like me, you rather enjoy a tart salad add segments of grapefruit from which all pith has been carefully removed. Top that blend with a few sprigs of watercress and you've a delightful cold weather salad.

'Witloof'

I've said that growing 'Witloof' chicory is a bother and one that few gardeners attempt, but anyone prepared to take a bit of trouble can certainly produce some luxury winter salad material at home this way and save considerably on the cost of buying.

The ideal site for chicory is on a medium-to-light soil manured for the previous crop – new manure can lead to forked roots that are of little use for lifting and blanching. Sow seed of the 'Witloof'-type in May in a ½ in-deep drill after raking 1 oz per sq yd of general fertiliser into the site and working soil down to a fine tilth. Once true leaves have appeared, thin the plants to 7 ins apart and then – apart from weeding, an occasional hoeing through and watering in dry spells – there's nothing to do until autumn. Leaves will die down in October to November and then you must lift the roots, discarding any that are thin or forked and saving those that resemble parsnips and are an inch or more across at the top.

Cut off the remaining leaves to ½ in from the crown, rub off any sideshoots and cut off root ends to leave an 8 or 9 ins length. Pack these roots on their sides in boxes of dry sand to store in a cool frost-free place until needed for forcing. To keep up a supply of chicons all through winter it's best to start blanching in mid-November and start a small batch every week until your supply runs out. Pack four or five of the prepared roots into a 9-ins flower pot filled with sand or light garden soil,

69

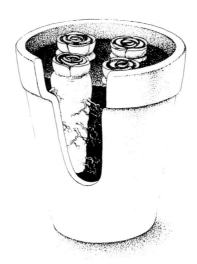

Figure 28: Packing 4-5 'Witloof' prepared roots in a 9-ins flower pot, to force

Figure 29: 'Sugar Loaf' plants growing in garden

with about $\frac{1}{2}$ in of root above the surface. Water sparingly and cover with an upturned pot of the same size, or with a black polythene bag, to exclude all light – allowing any light in will give green bitter leaves. Keep the soil or sand damp, but not wet, and stand pots in a well-ventilated and warm spot, which could be under the staging of a heated greenhouse, in a cellar, or in the cupboard under the stairs.

After about four weeks your first chicons should be ready to cut or snap off. Some people discard the roots right away, but if you keep them on there will be a crop of sideshoots that cut up splendidly in mixed salads.

'Sugar Loaf'

That is growing chicory the hard way and, by contrast, 'Sugar Loaf' – and similar varieties like 'Crystal Head', 'Winter Fare' and 'Snowflake' – are very easy. Prepare the site in the same way and give similar attention through the growing season. However, don't sow until the second half of June, or plants may run up to seed, and thin to 9 ins apart as the large heads need ample room to develop. I find this is a good crop to follow on after early lettuce grown on land manured in winter. By late October plants will have developed heads that look rather like giant cos lettuces and they are ready for cutting when they feel firm and solid if pressed with the back of your hand.

Strip off outer leaves to go on the compost heap and you'll be left with a great big chicon of pale creamy-green leaves that may weigh 2 lb, and will give delicious salad material for the family for several days. Store what is not needed in a plastic box in the fridge.

Unless we have exceptionally hard weather before Christmas, 'Sugar Loaf' and its sisters should go on into New Year. I've found that even when frost has spoilt the outer leaves there is a good heart to use in the kitchen, but as this chicory isn't all that hardy it is wise to throw some straw over the plants or cover with cloches through the worst of winter.

'Red Verona'

'Red Verona' chicory is so new to Britain that I can't give accurate advice on how well it will stand up to a hard winter, but it is very much hardier than 'Sugar Loaf' and something I'd recommend trying. Sow and grow in exactly the same way and don't be alarmed because summer leaves are green, for they won't turn to red until cold weather comes. Except, perhaps, in a very cold winter, this is a salad stuff to bring in fresh from the garden during those first months of the year when we all find it difficult to provide a good variety of salad ingredients.

If you've a small garden and little room for vegetables I think your precious space is far better given over to the cold weather salad crops that we seldom see in the shops, than to the cabbages and root crops that many British farmers grow. Trying something new makes salads much more interesting and, if you watch the seed catalogues, I feel sure you will find more and more of the Continental chicories being offered for home growing.

CHAPTER 10

Leaf Salads

If you are interested only in conventional lettuce, tomato and cucumber type salads you may want to skip part of this chapter. But if, like my family, you enjoy experimenting with different blends of unusual ingredients I'm certain that you'll enjoy trying green salads made from some of the leaves that are used widely on the Continent, but not very often in Britain.

Leaf Cress

You are sure to have eaten mustard and cress at one time or another, but if you rely on the shops it will almost certainly really have been the salad rape that grows more quickly and so is a better commercial proposition than the true mustard and cress. I'll deal with growing that along with sprouting seeds, but here I want to put in a word for *cress* grown until the ferny true leaves have developed.

I thought that was a leaf salad dreamed up by my old Kentish grandmother, who enjoyed raw green leaves so much that grandfather said she must be related to a rabbit! But recently I've discovered that true leaf cress is grown a great deal in Belgium, with patches in most gardens, though I'm still sure that my granny invented the salad for herself.

She sowed seeds in a broad shallow drill in odd spots near the garden path and waited until the cress had developed the curly true leaves that look rather like chervil. She gathered these one by one to mix into salads or use as sandwich fillings. Plants run up to seed quite soon, but given good ground and ample moisture give a good many pickings over two or three weeks. By sowing little and often it's very easy to keep up a supply through the warm months and because the crop develops so quickly, I find it a great boon in the spring period when we are waiting for slower-growing lettuce and other salads to mature and again in late summer if there looks like being a gap in lettuce production.

My grandmother grew her leaf cress only outside, but given protection of a cold house or cloches you can produce this easiest of all crops some weeks earlier; and because it's so economical of space and needs this for such a short time leaf cress could be produced by anyone.

These leaves have a stronger, hotter flavour than seed leaf cress, but when grown quickly with ample moisture are very tender and tasty. I serve them generously in with other leaf salads, or with sprouting broccoli tips, grated carrot and mung bean shoots.

Watercress

Watercress is something most of us buy from the shops, but few people attempt to grow it at home. A native plant of Britain, this can be found growing wild, but it's very unwise to gather this as the foliage is often mixed with that of poisonous weeds that look confusingly similar. Also, there is a danger that plants may be growing in contaminated water.

Watercress cultivated in pure water and eaten when fresh is a very nutritious salad stuff and is available through most of the year, but specially in spring, late summer and autumn. Known for centuries as a medicinal plant, watercress is a good source of vitamins A and C, is rich in iron, contains calcium, vitamin E and provides dietary fibre.

Buy only bunches that have a growers' label attached and see that the leaves are of a good rich green with no yellowing, wilting, nor with sideshoots attached to the stems. After well washing and draining, watercress can be stored in a plastic box in the salad drawer of the fridge, but because it's so much better when fresh I'd recommend liberal servings on the day of purchase.

Although commercial growers provide constant running water for their watercress beds, it is possible to grow in the garden if you can maintain a permanently damp situation. Healthy shoots from a shop bunch left in a glass of water will root after a week or so and can be planted in a shady damp part of the garden in early spring. To prepare the site, make a trench 2 ft wide and 1 ft deep, half fill with rotted manure or garden compost and then return 3-4 ins of soil. Plant rooted cuttings 6 ins apart, clip back to encourage bushy growth and water frequently. Remove flower stems when they appear and don't try to harvest too many sprigs from the perennial plants in their first year.

Land Cress

The American or *land cress* is a valuable leaf salad plant that tastes rather like watercress and is very easy to grow at home. You won't find this is the shops, nor in any conventional salad recipes, but I serve the rich-green tasty leaves liberally in green salads and we enjoy them as much as watercress.

Land cress needs a damp site, but no running water, and will thrive in any fertile soil that's never allowed to dry out. A biennial, it seeds itself and has formed a colony in one corner of my plastic tunnel house, which supplies us with many bunches of fresh foliage through the colder months and especially in those first weeks of spring when growth is rapid under plastic, but the weather is too cold for any fresh salad stuff to be available from the open garden.

You can sow in March in the open and in succession through the warm months, but I believe the most important sowing is that made in late summer to cover with cloches or protect in some other way through winter. If you've no cloches or frame you can protect the row with wooden planks placed

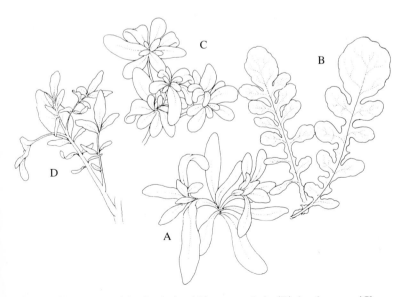

Figure 30: Assorted leaf salads: (A) corn salad, (B) land cress, (C) purslane, (D) salad rocket

on edge and held in position with short pegs along both sides of the row and with odd sheets of glass on top to give a makeshift frame. If you have a greenhouse, but no border, this is a useful candidate for sowing in the open in August to transplant into growing bags vacated by tomatoes or cucumbers in October.

Thin or transplant land cress to about 4 ins apart each way to make rosettes of rich-green shiny foliage, removing flower stems as they appear and picking regularly to encourage the appearance of more fresh succulent leaves. Never allow the soil round the roots to become dry and if you are doubtful of soil fertility, add some liquid feed to the water from time to time. Pick leaves one by one, wash under the tap, and serve whole in any kind of mixed salad, or use as a topping for other ingredients.

Corn Salad

Corn salad, sometimes called lamb's lettuce, is a leaf salad much appreciated on the Continent, but not often grown in this country and something I can't imagine finding on sale in any shop. Again, it is a plant you can sow in succession through the warm months, but one I sow in August to grow on *in situ* under cloches or transplant to the border or to once-used growing bags in my cold greenhouse or plastic tunnel for protection from mid-autumn until we've an abundance of salad stuffs in the open six months later.

Thinned or transplanted to 4 ins apart each way, corn salad makes rosettes of leaves rather like those of a forget-me-not in shape but with a shiny green surface. Gather them individually, wash and serve freely in green salads or use as a topping for a mixed salad bowl.

Plants left in the open uncovered will come on in spring, but I think protection is advisable because it is in cold weather that we need fresh green leaves most. Even in snowy spells, when cabbages were buried under a white blanket and stored roots and onions gave the only choice of vegetables for cooking, I've been able to go into my plastic tunnel house to gather a dish full of land cress, corn salad and other leafy plants.

As with all plants that you want to keep on making new tender leaves, fertile soil is needed and ample moisture to give lush foliage, but for corn salad good drainage is also important.

Chervil

Chervil is a herb that I always grow alongside my corn salad, for the ferny little leaves with a flavour reminiscent of aniseed are something we like to use in the same way, though with more discretion than those of the milder leaf salads. I sow this easy hardy annual in spring too so that I can use the tasty leaves to pep up mixed salads through summer, and because the plants quickly run up to seed I find it best to plant a short row thinned to 3 ins apart every month.

Chervil is a herb that was used to impart what Parkinson, a seventeenth-century herbalist, described as a sweet, pleasant and hot spicy taste to salads in the days before lettuce was much grown. I think it's a pity the plant went out of fashion and if you like variety, I'm sure you will enjoy the curly leaves in your salads.

Parsley

Parsley is another herb that I include among leaf salads because the curly nutritious foliage is so good to eat either broken into sprigs and mixed into the salad bowl or finely chopped and used as a topping. A biennial to sow in April and

Figure 31: Parsley: (summer) outside in a row, (winter) in a large pot in a greenhouse

perhaps again at midsummer, this needs a fertile soil that's never allowed to dry out and thrives in semi-shade. Ideally, grow the herb near a path so picking is easy in all weathers, either in a row or in a patch about 2 ft wide, so you can reach right across to gather leaves from the back.

To maintain a supply through winter cloche your parsley in the open, or pot up some thinnings from the late row to grow in the greenhouse or on a windowsill indoors – a 9-ins pot should take three plants and, given ample water and a bit of liquid feed, will supply a good amount of foliage. In the garden, treat them well so growth is rapid and leaves tender, picking over the plants regularly so plenty of new leaves come – in spring pinch out flower buds from last year's sowing so the parsley goes on until the new season's sowing is ready to harvest.

Seed is slow to germinate and I reckon to sow a few radish seeds in the same drill so they act as row markers and give a catch crop before the herb plants have reached true leaf stage and need thinning to 6 ins apart. Keep the seed bed moist and water regularly through dry spells.

Curly parsley leaves are rich in iron and vitamins. You can buy bunches in the shops and keep fairly fresh by standing in a glass of water in a cool place. But, even in the smallest garden, you should be able to keep up a supply so your family can enjoy the foliage at its freshest and most nutritious. 'Moss Curled' has long been the best-known variety, but try too the newer 'Bravour' and 'Consort'.

French Sorrel

French sorrel is a better-class relation of the wild sorrel that grows freely in British meadowland. Leaves are larger and more succulent, less acid in flavour and of a paler green. You won't want to serve them too liberally, but one or two torn up or cut with the kitchen scissors are splendid blended in with more generous helpings of other leaf salads.

A perennial, this likes a sunny spot on rich land and can be raised from seed sown in April and thinned to 8 ins apart, or increased by splitting off a bit from an established plant in early spring. Water well in dry weather. Leaves appear early in spring and are at their best in the warm months.

Purslane

Purslane is a half-hardy annual that was once a popular salad plant in this country and is widely grown across the Channel for serving in spring and summer salads, but is now almost a stranger to Britain.

Sow in light but good soil under cloches in April and in monthly succession from May on in the open, choosing a sunny position. A cousin of the *Portulaca* of our flower gardens, this has round fleshy dark-green leaves on red stems. Gather them individually and remove flower stems as they emerge. On the Continent you'll find patches a yard or so across in many gardens, for there they appreciate mixtures of all these small salad leaves.

Winter purslane, or *Claytonia*, comes from America and is very hardy. Sow thinly in rows or a patch in July or August and thin to 4 ins apart to give leaves for cold weather salads.

Salad Rocket

Another leaf salad popular across the Channel, but no longer grown much in this country, is *salad rocket*, which shouldn't be confused with the sweet rocket of our flower gardens. This is an annual with peppery little leaves that look a bit like those of land cress and have a flavour that's earned the plant the name of mustard herb in Germany. Not widely available from seed firms in Britain, this is well worth trying if you like experimenting with different plants to make your salads more interesting.

Sow in a cold greenhouse in February to give a patch with young leaves for cutting in spring, then in the open to follow on.

Dandelion

You may not be familiar with some of the plants I've described, but everyone knows the *dandelion*. That's a weed that we all try to eradicate from our lawns and borders, but it's also a most valuable leaf salad in the spring.

I suppose you could cultivate the wild plants, but it's far better to sow seed of the thick-leaved strain. Do this in April, sowing on fertile soil in a row or patch and thinning seedlings to 9 ins apart so they develop into big succulent plants. The

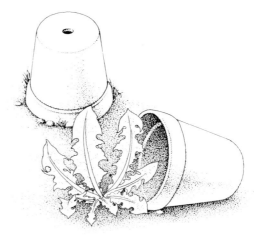

Figure 32: Dandelion plants being forced *in situ* for blanched spring leaves

leaves will die down in autumn, but the crowns of the plant will still be visible and come February I cover them individually with upturned 9-ins flower pots to encourage growth and blanch the long leaves. If you want really pale foliage you must place a bit of crock or a stone over the drainage hole in each pot, but I prefer the slightly green leaves that come when a little light is allowed in. Rather than cover one plant at a time, you can grow in a small patch and cover with an upturned wooden box or an old tub, planning the patch to fit the cover that is available.

The first year that I grew dandelions I was amazed at the number of leaves produced from a dozen or so plants over some weeks of spring and early summer. They are perennial, but I find they are pretty exhausted after one season and prefer to start a new batch every year. This is a salad that's specially good for heavy land and, like other leaf salads, needs ample moisture for best results.

Gather as many leaves as you need for one meal, wash under the tap, and serve whole or broken up in a blend of leafy ingredients; or serve whole as you would watercress along with lettuce and more conventional salad stuffs.

Chop Suey Greens

Most of the leaf salads come from across the Channel, but it is to the Orient that we look for *chop suey greens* to give deeply-cut, aromatic, bright-green foliage. An easily-grown member of the chrysanthemum family, this makes plants that look rather like feverfew and in about six weeks from sowing in warmer weather will give leaves to cut for salads, or in Chinese style to fry in oil. Sow in succession from April on in drills 1 in deep, thin to about 4 ins apart, water well, and gather leaves individually when about 4 ins high.

If you rely on the shops, these are just a few of the health-giving and tasty salad stuffs that will seldom if ever be on your family's menu; so if your garden is small I'd suggest devoting precious space to these less common plants and buying in those produced by all the commercial growers.

CHAPTER 11

The Cabbage Family

The cabbage family is very important to anyone who serves salads regularly, for the different members provide so much variety – and one or other of them is available right through the year.

Even in a small plot I couldn't bear to be without a cabbage patch of some kind, and when I plan my succession to crop through the year I choose varieties as much for eating raw as for cooking, giving priority to those that don't travel well to market or are unpopular with commercial growers for some other reason.

Historical Background

Modern brassicas look very different but, whether tight button sprouts, curly kale or cauliflower, they have all been derived from the wild cabbage that grows on the White Cliffs of Dover and at other places around our seashores.

The Brussels sprout is believed to have originated in Belgium and has been known there since the thirteenth century. It is my favourite of the family for salads, for eaten whole or shredded raw sprouts are so delicious and so nutritious.

The family is a good source of vitamin C, Brussels sprouts being particularly valuable for supplying this in winter when we all want to ward off colds and infections. But much goodness is lost in cooking, or when leaves have been cut long enough to wilt, and so serving raw and fresh in salads is most beneficial. Raw newly gathered Brussels sprouts contain up to five times as much vitamin C as boiled cabbage. They, and the other members of the family, also contain significant amounts of potassium and phosphorus, as well as minerals and protein.

The Cabbage Family

All the cabbage family need a fertile soil and are best moved around the plot so they are not grown on the same land more than once in three years. In a three-year rotation of crops they should follow peas, beans and other vegetables grown the previous season on land supplied with rotted manure or garden compost. The legumes leave nitrogen in the ground to help feed the cabbages. If your soil is at all acid, an application of lime in the winter before planting is of help, but you won't need that if, like me, you are on chalky land.

All brassicas need firm ground and that's specially so of the Brussels sprout which, if the soil is loose and fluffy, may produce blown open sprouts instead of the tight buttons we want. I've known some gardeners go over the site with the garden roller before planting, but as much of my gardening life has been on clay that wasn't necessary and I'd have thought treading the ground around individual plants when they are put in should always firm sufficiently.

With a few exceptions all the cabbage family are sown in seed beds to be transplanted when they have developed into good sturdy plants of around 6 ins high. You can sow all the main brassicas at one time in late March to early April in a seed bed in the open, but I sow mine over some months in batches to give the widest possible selection. The first sowings are made under glass in late January to early February, a second batch goes under cloches or in my plastic tunnel house early in March and then there is a series of outdoor sowings. Seeds of this family stay viable for two to three years and so long as you make sure the date is clearly marked on the packet – the seedsman's date is so often torn off during opening – and stale seed is used first, each variety can be relied on to do for at least two seasons.

You can, of course, buy in plants, but seeds are so easy to raise that I'd hate to do that and, anyway, garden shops seldom offer all the varieties I want. If you do buy look out for fresh and green plants of good size with well developed roots; once home, stand the bundles in water up to the lower leaves for a good drink before planting.

Water your own seed bed overnight unless there has been recent rain so plants come up easily with good unbroken roots. Ideally transplanting should be done in showery weather, but as that's not always possible aim for evening planting and thorough watering to achieve a quick getaway. In very hot weather one friend of mine protects her newly-planted brassicas from the sun with shades made from rhubarb or mature cabbage leaves propped up by bits of twig. Alteratively, you can make shades from sheets of newspaper.

Brussels Sprouts

I sow my early *Brussels sprouts* in the tunnel house, or under cloches, at the beginning of March and follow on with a later variety sown in the open a month afterwards. Because wild birds are so partial to newly germinated brassica seedlings, the outdoor drill is protected with plastic fruit netting or black thread stretched between short sticks at either end. The seedsmen keep on bringing out new Brussels sprouts, many of the F_1 hybrids popular with commercial growers because all the buttons form at roughly the same time and plants can be picked over just once or cut to sell on the stick. Some gardeners say that they prefer the older varieties that cropped over a longer period, but I've found the modern hybrids will stay in good condition for a long while and like them for their vigour, uniformity and quality.

Figure 33: Shredding Brussels sprouts for salad

For the early harvest I've not found a better one than 'Peer Gynt' and, as this is of dwarf habit, plants can go out at little more than 2 ft apart – older taller varieties needed at least 30 ins each way – fit into small gardens and are far less likely to blow over in autumn winds. In an exposed garden, or where growth is particularly good, you need to stake or earth up taller sprout plants, or they will lean over at all kinds of nasty angles. 'Peer Gynt' is ready to pick in October and continues to crop for several months, with firm buttons ideal for shredding raw. You can follow on with mid and late season varieties, but I think two sorts is ample in most gardens and so I follow on with 'Perfect Line', 'Citadel', or one of the other F_1 hybrids recommended for gathering between Christmas and March. For novelty effect and adding something different to salads you might like to try the variety 'Rubine' with dark red buttons of good quality. They look delightful shredded with chopped chicory and celery.

I try to transplant my early Brussels sprouts by the middle of June and if space is available they go in at the end of May; while the late row goes out by early July at the latest. Many people like to plant with a dibber, but I much prefer a trowel, as this allows a wider hole to spread out the roots. Plant with lower leaves at soil level, fill the hole in with soil and firm well with the heel of your boot or shoe, tugging a leaf to make sure the plant is well anchored and filling the hole made with your heel with water to make sure roots are moist right away.

Never let any newly-planted brassicas dry out until they are starting to make new growth. As plants don't go out until at least the end of May the site can be used first for an early salad crop, perhaps cloched lettuce, radish and spring onions, or carrots for May pulling. After these plants have been cleared the site will need forking over and I like to rake in a dressing of 2 ozs of general fertiliser to each sq yd.

If cabbage root fly is a problem in your garden you may feel it necessary to dust Bromophos around the base of each newly-planted brassica, but if you like to avoid chemical control you may prefer to fit collars of tarred paper, roofing felt or carpet underlay around the stems of the plants. Research has shown that circles about 5 ins in diameter cut from any of these materials and slit from one side to the centre so they can be fitted round the plants helps prevent fly trouble, because the female cannot lay her eggs in the soil by the base of the stem.

After your Brussels sprouts have been planted they won't need a lot of attention until harvest, apart from weeding and occasional hoeing, but do water generously in dry spells and with taller varieties or in exposed gardens earth up the stems lightly a month after the move. In autumn, remove lower yellowing leaves to let in light and air and always start picking from the bottom of the stem upwards. Rather than leave any loose blown sprouts I gather these early on for stews, or if they are very messy add them to the compost heap.

Brussels sprouts are in season from September to March and, whereas a cabbage may become stale before all is used, you can gather just a few or as many buttons as you need for a family meal or an individual serving. Trim off outer leaves, wash well and serve whole with wholemeal bread and cheese and celery, or shredded with almost any blend of autumn or winter salad ingredients. The tops are good too, and although I use most for cooking I'll usually ease out the tenderest centre part for salad use. Cutting them early in the season encourages the plants to button up, but I prefer to leave mine until after Christmas, making sure they are cut before the hardest January weather comes, because tops are often spoiled by hard frost or by pigeons driven into the garden by wintry conditions and shortage of food in the wild.

Sprouting Broccoli

For late winter and spring salads I find *sprouting broccoli* an exceptionally useful brassica and as it's also one of my favourite cooked vegetables a row is high on my priority list. You can usually buy decent cabbage from the shops, but I've never yet been tempted by any sample of sprouting broccoli, for commercial growers cut it in large sections, with coarse leaves and these wither too soon to look appetising a day after gathering. At home, on the other hand, you can go along with the colander and snip out just the tender little shoots you want for eating raw or cooking, with no further need to trim once indoors.

Purple sprouting is such an accommodating crop for the garden. Seed is sown from mid-April to mid-May to give plants to go out from late June and they'll start to crop at New Year and go on well into spring. As with other brassicas, it's best to sow thinly and if seedlings still come up thickly you want to pull out the weakest once true leaves have formed, leaving seedlings 1 in apart so each can develop into a sturdy young plant. Drills in the seed bed should be $\frac{1}{2}$-in deep and about 6 ins apart.

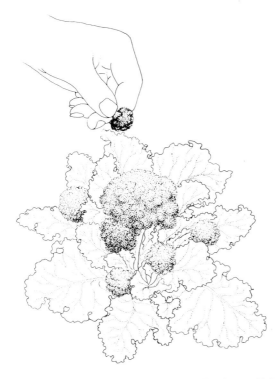

Figure 34: Picking tiny spears of purple sprouting broccoli for salads

I've often found that the most valuable purple sprouting comes from a late row put in during the first week of August, for by then there is more room for new plants because many early vegetables have been harvested and, given plenty of water in the next few weeks to ensure a quick getaway, plants are large enough to give a high yield in those lean weeks of spring when fresh foodstuff is more scarce. Suttons offer early and late varieties of purple sprouting, but I grow just the one recommended for mid-season and offered by every seed house.

There is also a white sprouting broccoli that comes mid-season and many believe is of superior flavour, though plants do not give such a high yield. I don't usually grow that, but I must admit the smaller white spears are most delectable in a salad if gathered from the garden and used right away.

All the sprouting broccoli varieties are liable to succumb to very hard winter weather, especially if you treat them too well, and so I like to grow mine in better drained parts of the garden and away from any low-lying spot that may be a frost pocket. Don't be put off by tales of almost all plants being killed off by the hard winter of 1978/9, because though statistics have been published, quoting only 40 surviving plants in commercial holdings and private gardens, I had nearly 20 purple sprouting plants that came through on an exposed hilltop in East Kent and to the best of my belief and knowledge these were never counted.

Prepare the site for the crop as that for Brussels sprouts, put plants in at 2 ft each way and, especially with the later row and in dry spells, be very generous with water after planting out. Come late February, I give my sprouting broccoli a spring fillip of 1 oz per sq yd of nitro-chalk or nitrate of soda, hoe this in and with longer warmer days growth soon comes on apace. Pigeons can be a menace with the crop in some seasons and so it pays to be ready with some plastic fruit netting to cover plants as soon as you see the birds have moved in.

Never cut larger pieces than you need for table, as new shoots will form in leaf axils and so cutting too deeply can reduce the overall crop. Use larger, leafier centre pieces and sideshoots for cooking and all the tenderest little sprigs for eating raw. They are delicious and nutritious blended with such seasonal salad ingredients as finely grated carrot, early leaf salads, sprouted seeds or diced apple. As the season progresses and days become warmer, buds will quickly open to flowers and picking should keep ahead of this, even if you have to throw away some bits, for once a plant has flowered there will seldom be many new shoots.

Kale

There are several kinds of *kale*, but just one that I grow for salad use. This is a comparatively new hybrid between the curly and plain leaved types that was raised by researchers in Scotland and given the name 'Pentland Brig'. I sow it at the same time and give plants the same treatment as sprouting broccoli, and am rewarded with lots of slightly curly leaves for cooking from Christmas to late April and also with many gatherings of small tender sideshoots that develop in the leaf axils and are so good raw that my family would hate to see them go in a saucepan.

Again, you won't find a good sample in the shops and so 'Pentland Brig' kale is a crop you must grow for yourself. I think that this and the other cut-and-come-again brassicas for eating raw are so much more important in a limited area than those that make just one big head. But, of course, I grow various cabbages too, usually saving the best from the centre of a head prepared to cook with the Sunday roast for shredding raw to go with cold meat in Monday's salad. Washed and stowed away in the fridge in a plastic box raw cabbage will keep for several days, but as it's so much best when fresh, it's wiser to buy or try and grow smaller heads rather than those weighing several pounds apiece.

Cabbage

One *cabbage* or another is in season in every month and when working out my cropping programme I aim at producing a continuous supply, for with no more land and a bit of forethought you can harvest one or two a week all year rather than have a series of gluts and shortages because too many of one type were planted together. Swopping plants or seeds with friends, or making each packet do for two or three years, allows you to grow a wide selection for a well-planned succession without a big outlay.

My first sowing is made in late January in gentle heat with a thin sprinkling of seeds going in a seed pan of John Innes seed compost. When well up the infant plants are pricked out into the border of my cold greenhouse – they could go in a growing bag if you have no border – to give plants to go out under cloches in March. That may sound rather a bother for cabbages, but those very first summer cabbage are so welcome and come so quickly that the extra care is justified. Another sowing of the same variety is made in February in the cold greenhouse border, or in my plastic tunnel house to give plants to go out in the open in April. For both I'll use the pointed F_1 hybrid 'Hispi', or ball-headed 'Golden Acre Progress', and a further modest sowing of either of these in the open in March continues the succession.

Don't get the idea that I grow a vast number of cabbages at any one time, for I prefer to have a few to cut every week from early June to September, with batches of perhaps ten plants, rather than to plant one long row of summer cabbages that split and end up on the compost heap because they all come together when there's a glut of other vegetables. Surplus plants find a ready sale and help pay my seed bill, especially if they are available before many other gardeners have any ready to transplant. A 12-15 ins square plant gives ample space for these compact varieties.

An April sowing of the F_1 hybrid 'Minicole' gives Dutch white-type solid heads with thick meaty flesh to use through late summer and until autumn frosts come. They'll stand in good condition for some weeks without splitting and are often recommended for small families because of the modest size. You will only achieve small heads on fertile soil, however, if you use a 10-ins square plant, for trials have shown that a conventional 2-ft square plant will give heads weighing several pounds apiece.

'Holland Late Winter' gives a similar type of head that's heavy and solid, and very good for coleslaw. It is one of a number of Dutch white-type cabbages that won't stand much frost and so are normally cut in November to store in dry airy conditions for winter use. I never grow them, partly because the heads are readily available in the shops, but largely because I believe cabbage should be eaten fresh and so there can be little goodness in one that's been kept in a shed for weeks. Also, my family much prefer a savoy cooked or shredded and eaten raw to these thick meaty cabbages, and this can be brought in from the garden or will have been cut from a farm field right through the cold months.

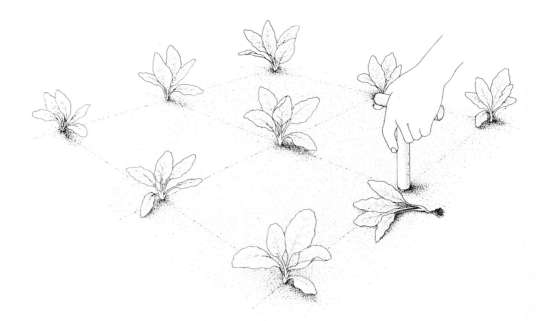

Figure 35: 'Minicole' cabbage, going in at 10 ins square plant, to give modest heads

Savoys

Savoys for autumn cutting are sown in late April in the open and transplanted in late June at 2 ft each way on a site prepared as for Brussels sprouts and other summer planted brassicas. I've not found a better variety than the old and very well-named 'Best of All'. Don't sow before late April or heads will come in when you've still plenty of summer vegetables. I like to aim for the first savoys around the third week of October.

To follow on there's that good old standby 'January King' that puts up with hard weather well, or even better the F_1 hybrid 'Aquarius' of the same type that stands for a long time and because of its compact habit can be planted a bit closer. Sow either in May for a July move.

None of the savoys are the type of cabbage you normally find in coleslaw, but shredded up for a salad base topped by finely grated carrot, diced or sliced apple, chopped celery and almost any other blend of winter ingredients you can think of, they make a perfect accompaniment to cold meat, or cheese and hard-boiled egg.

If you buy these or other cabbages, look first for freshness with no withered or yellowed outer leaves, then for a firm solid heart with few outside leaves that will push the scales up unnecessarily. The best place to buy is from a farm shop that's supplied direct from the fields, for here freshness is guaranteed and price really competitive.

You might think it odd to recommend pickling cabbage for eating raw, but when shredded the heart gives a welcome change of flavour and colour and is well worth trying. A rather longer growing season is needed and so you need to sow quite early in spring to transplant 12 ins apart each way in May for a dwarf variety like 'Niggerhead' to cut in autumn. Heads won't stand a lot of frost, but can be stored like the winter whites. Readily available from greengrocery shops, red cabbages are often sold in sections if you want to experiment with just a quarter or half.

To complete my succession of cabbages for eating right through the year there are the spring-heading varieties (that form their heads in the spring) that we sow in late July and early August to transplant in late September and early October for maturing next season. With these you give no fertiliser at planting time, but a dose of nitrate of soda or one of the other quick-acting nitrogenous fertilisers in late February to push growth along as warmer weather returns. A foot each way is ample room and putting plants in at 6 ins apart in the row, with alternate ones cut as winter greens next February, is a popular method of space-saving. Given a good start with sturdy plants put out at Michaelmas you should be cutting in April or early May. Some varieties are large and leafy, but others small and conical with few outer leaves and these are the best if you want early maturity and good hearts for shredding raw in salads. 'April' and 'Offenham Spring Bounty' are two good varieties. Newer and highly recommended in the catalogues is the F_1 hybrid round 'Spring Hero' that stands well without splitting, is very early and very hardy, and a most unusual shape for a spring cabbage.

Pigeons are the very devils on over-wintering cabbage plants and I believe plastic fruit netting is the best way of keeping them off the bed in the hardest winter weather. In colder districts, cloches will help growth, give protection from the elements and prevent bird damage.

Of course, there are dozens of other cabbage varieties, but I've just picked out my favourites to give a selection right through the year, so shredded cabbage is always available to make the base of my salads.

Cauliflower

Before finishing with the cabbage family I must say something about the *cauliflower*. This isn't a plant I'd grow just for salad use, but what I tend to do is to save a few sprigs from a curd when I'm preparing our favourite cauliflower cheese, to stow away in the fridge for mixing in next day's salad.

You can produce cauliflower all through the year, but I seldom serve this raw in the months when we've a vast choice of salad ingredients. I'm therefore only going to discuss growing the late winter and spring crop that I believe is far the most valuable for salads and for cooking. This is the most difficult time to produce good hearted cabbages and most other fresh vegetables are at a premium and so a row of cauliflowers is a valuable investment.

These cauliflowers that grow through the coldest months don't need such fertile conditions as those that mature in summer and autumn and because heavy, damp soil can lead to winter losses they are best grown where drainage is good.

Sow seed from mid-April to mid-May for transplanting in late June and July into a site prepared as for Brussels sprouts with 2 ft each way between plants. Cauliflowers hate to be checked so it is never wise to stint water, either in the seed bed or in the row, particularly in the first weeks after transplanting. When curds begin to swell protect them from weather by snapping off one or two big leaves so they bend over the centre of the plant. Cauliflowers are more prone to root fly trouble than most other brassicas, so collars around the stems at planting, or a dusting with Bromophos, are sensible precautions.

Among varieties I don't think you'll go far wrong with are 'Angers No. 2 Westmarsh Early' for February and March eating: 'Angers No. 2 Snow White' to go on into April; 'Walcheren Winter Birchington' to take you into late April and early May; and 'Walcheren Winter Manston' to go on to later May.

If you buy cauliflowers in spring or at any other season, look for clean white curds that have not started to open out, fresh green leaves and, for the best buy, go to farm shops or market stalls supplied direct from the fields.

You'll see from all this that, for me, the cabbage patch is an important part of the garden for salad production as well as to give vegetables for cooking. I think you'll see too that coleslaw is by no means the only way of serving the cabbage tribe raw, but that your salads can be more exciting if you experiment with serving these nutritious and delicious greens in a variety of ways.

CHAPTER 12

The Oriental Influence

Chinese Cabbage

In recent years the plant breeders have given us a number of F_1 hybrid forms of the *Chinese cabbage* to make an exciting addition to our range of salad ingredients. Grown in Asia for many hundreds of years, but not introduced to Europe until the turn of the century, the Chinese cabbage of a few years back was a much greener and looser-leaved vegetable than the pale firm heads of the new hybrids.

Mainly during autumn and early winter you can find them in the more discerning greengrocery shops, but they look so unlike our British cabbage that you could be forgiven for thinking there was no relationship. In fact, the Chinese cabbage is more closely related to the turnip than to our cabbage. You can cook the heads, but it is for salad use that the modern forms are so very good. They look rather like giant cos lettuce with crinkled savoy-like leaves and are superb for shredding to blend with finely grated carrot, chopped celery, sliced winter radish and other crunchy cold weather salad stuffs. If you buy, look out for fresh crisp heads that feel firm and solid, avoiding those with any hint of withering or that feel soft and flabby.

Because they have quite a short growing season, Chinese cabbages are easy to fit into the cropping programme, following on after July harvested beans, peas or other vegetables grown on land manured the previous winter. Sow immediately these have been cleared and the new crop itself will be cleared in time for the site to be winter dug in readiness for next spring's sowings.

Rake in a dressing of general fertiliser when preparing the site and if you decide on land that has not been fed with humus in the last twelve months, work in also a bucketful of well-rotted garden compost to every square yard.

This is a vegetable that needs a really fertile soil and must have ample moisture, and so you have to be generous with water from sowing right through the early weeks in most seasons. On drier soils you'll find it helps if you can add a bucketful of peat to the square yard, perhaps making use of a growing bag already used for last summer's tomatoes and then for early spring salad crops. Without being so heavy on peat, you can assist germination with this and other summer sowings by taking out extra deep drills and lining them with moist peat before the seeds go in.

Chinese cabbage doesn't transplant too well and so it's best to sow thinly and thin seedlings to 12-15 ins apart to grow on *in situ*. That may sound rather a lot of room, but some varieties make very big heads, the F_1 hybrid 'Nagoaka' producing whoppers weighing 4-5 lb that will supply salad meals for a family for several days. With 'Minicole' cabbage I advise close spacing to prevent over-sized heads, but with these you need to give space and part of the reason for weight is that plants are tall with barrel-shaped heads when leaves have turned in.

Some of the F_1 hybrids are resistant to bolting, but on the whole it's wiser not to sow before July and in any case I think the main value of the crop is to come in during autumn after summer lettuce is but a memory. Trials at the Royal Horticultural Society gardens at Wisley a few years ago showed that the third week in July was the best time and that's usually when we are ready to clear away early summer vegetables for a follow-on. If your previous planting has not been harvested by then don't despair, for I've done very well with 1 August sowing.

This is a very quick crop and given ample moisture and good soil you should be able to start cutting heads in ten weeks from sowing. Chinese cabbage will stand until January if weather is good, but won't put up with harsh wet conditions. If your row contains more plants than you need for eating before Christmas, I'd advise covering with cloches on a day when leaves are dry to protect them from the elements and extend the season into New Year.

'Sugar Loaf' chicory comes in at the same time and has heads getting on for the same size, but whereas I've never found that troubled by slugs they can be an awful nuisance with Chinese cabbage and it's essential to put down regular supplies of slug killer – well protected from pets and wild birds – or the leaves may be ravaged by the pests who share our love for the succulent heads.

If heads seem loose, you can assist hearting up by raising

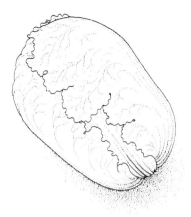

Figure 36: Chinese cabbage of 'Sampan' type

outer leaves and tying a couple of strands of raffia or soft twine around each plant, but that isn't always necessary. If you decide to do so, make sure leaves are dry, or you may introduce wet and decay.

Most seed firms offer only one or two forms of the Chinese cabbage and among the best are the F_1 hybrids 'Sampan', 'Nagoaka' and 'Tip Top No. 12'. Chiltern Seeds specialise in Oriental vegetables and offer a bigger range that includes the open pollinated 'Market Prider', and ball-shaped 'Che-foo' that has colossal heads weighing up to 6 lbs apiece. Watch the seed catalogues and I'm certain you'll find more and more varieties of this valuable Oriental brassica being offered to home gardeners.

Japanese Greens

If you enjoy experimenting with excitingly different salad crops, do look through the Chiltern Seeds catalogue and try some of their other plants from the Orient. One such is the Mizuna form of *Japanese greens*, a mustard that is resistant to cold and in its native land is grown extensively in winter.

A vigorous grower that produces clumps 8-12 ins across, this has dark-green, deeply-cut and fringed leaves with white stalks to cut off time and again as new foliage develops. Sow in spring, summer or autumn, to start picking in around six weeks and keep on cutting as needed indoors for quite some while.

96

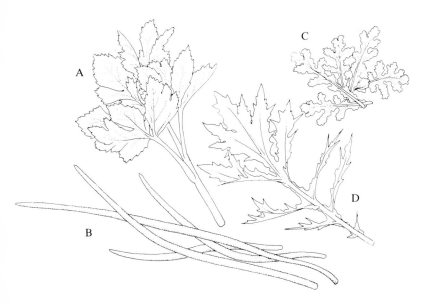

Figure 37: Assortment of Oriental salads: (A) Japanese parsley (Mitsuba), (B) broad-leaved Chinese chives, (C) chop suey greens, (D) Mizuna Japanese greens

Older foliage will be too tough to eat raw, but given a bit of protection through the worst weather, plants will give new leaves for salads until the end of winter.

Chop Suey Greens

In the chapter on leaf salads I included *chop suey greens*, a form of the annual chrysanthemum, to sow in autumn or spring to make clumps of aromatic deeply-cut foliage. Given protection of cloches or a tunnel house, this is another valuable cut-and-come-again Oriental salad stuff for cold weather meals.

Japanese Parsley

The Japanese parsley, Mitsuba, is a perennial with long tender leaf stalks each topped by three heart-shaped leaves. You can earth up the plants to give longer blanched and more succulent stems for salad eating.

97

Broad-leaved Chinese Chives

Broad-leaved Chinese chives (called also Chinese leeks) is a handsome perennial with leaves that have a garlic flavour and can be chopped to take the place of our much smaller chives. The dainty white flowers are also edible and can be used to garnish the salad bowl, and the bulbs are also good to eat.

These are just a few suggestions for unusual plants from the Orient to add variety to our salads. Perhaps you will feel some are a bit too different, but if you enjoy raw meals I'm positive you'll find shredded Chinese cabbage a must for autumn salads once you've given the modern hybrid forms a trial. Except in Chinese shops, probably only to be found in London and larger towns, you are unlikely to find any of the other plants I've discussed on sale, but they are not difficult to cultivate at home and won't demand very much room in your garden.

CHAPTER 13

Sprouting Seeds

Most of the salad plants described here came to us from the Orient and could have been included in the last chapter, but I felt that they deserved to be on their own because they are of such enormous value to any lover of raw food. Included too are our very English mustard and cress, two salad plants that are normally eaten as sprouting seeds that have developed just a little further to the seed leaf stage.

Of all the other sprouting seeds, by far the best known is the mung bean and this is now quite readily available from supermarkets and greengrocers. It's so easy to raise at home and is the quickest of all salad stuffs to produce, and so I'd consider this a real must. When you have tried the shoots, do go on to experiment with the full range of these delicious and very nutritious salad crops.

The Chinese cook bean shoots and no doubt some of the others could be treated this way, but they are so good raw that I much prefer to serve sprouted seeds in salads, and in uncooked sandwich fillings.

Around 5,000 years ago a Chinese emperor wrote a book on plants that referred to health-giving sprouts; it is only, however, in recent research that we have learned how much goodness is released once a seed starts to germinate. Once the sprouting process has begun, stored foods from the dormant seed are turned into nutrients readily absorbed by our bodies, and a sprouting seed will contain large amounts of vitamins A, B and C; far larger amounts than are initially present in the seed alone. The sprouting seeds are also very rich in proteins and such minerals as iron, calcium, potassium and iodine. Eat them raw at their prime and you've a wealth of nourishment.

You can produce these quick salad ingredients all year round, but they are of special value in those months of winter and early spring when there is a shortage of fresh food and we all need extra vitamins to help ward off colds, chills and other infections. Ready in just a few days from starting, sprouting seeds are best produced in small quantities right through the period, so that they can be eaten at the peak of perfection and give a constant supply of essential nutrients.

I've said that you can buy mung bean shoots, and these can be stored in the fridge for several days, but there's no need for anyone to buy because they are so very easy to raise in a warm cupboard at home. Whether you buy, or produce yourself, sprouting seeds should be rinsed thoroughly in cold water to remove any ungerminated seeds and seed coats from those that have developed shoots. With something as large as a mung bean, rinsing under the cold tap in a colander is the best way and you'll find that spare seed coats tend to go to the bottom, but with finer shoots like alfalfa I find it better to tip them out into a fine sieve. With these fine shoots you cannot remove every seed coat, but they are so small that they can easily be chewed up.

You can buy special containers for sprouting seeds, but that's not necessary for all the equipment you really need is a 2 lb jam jar, a piece of butter muslin or gauze and a stout elastic band to hold that in place. As you'll almost certainly want to have more than one batch of seeds coming along at one time it's best to have two or three jam jars and covers on the go.

Mung Beans

I've found that *mung beans* are the easiest and quickest of all the seeds to sprout, with some shoots ready to eat in just four or five days. With them, and even more with the smaller seeds, you must take care to start only a small quantity, as it's surprising how volume increases as the germination process gets under way.

With mung beans, two level tablespoons of seeds is ample to start with. Place these in the bottom of the jam jar, half fill this with cold water and leave overnight for the seeds to swell and start to split their seed coats. Next day tip the seeds into a sieve and rinse well under the cold tap, put them back in the jar with just a very little water, cover with muslin or gauze and then lie the jar on its side in a warm dark cupboard. There should be just enough water to keep the seeds damp, but not enough to run out when the jar is lying down.

The secret of successful seed sprouting is to rinse and re-dampen the seeds every twelve hours, for left alone for a whole day or more there is a risk of mould setting in, or of the top seeds drying out and an uneven sample developing with

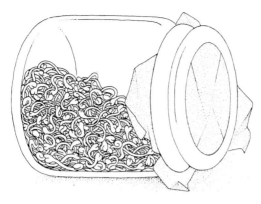

Figure 38: 2 lb jam jar on side, with mung beans sprouting inside

many wasted seeds that have not germinated and other shoots in varying stages of growth.

It only takes a few seconds night and morning to rinse the seeds during sprouting time if you run the cold tap through the gauze covering the jar, tip the water out and repeat several times. This helps to shake up the seeds so that all have a chance to be moistened evenly and there will be enough water in the jar to ensure that none dry out before the next treatment. If you are very busy, I find it pays to write a note on the kitchen jotter as a reminder about the jars of seeds at the beginning of the season, and that once I'm into batch after batch I remember quite easily.

Mung beans are very easy, for they are easily shaken up and don't grow into a tangled mass, but some of the finer shoots of other seeds become so tangled that once during the sprouting process I usually tip the contents of the jar into a sieve so that I can sort out the mass of growth. Mung beans are ready to eat the quickest, but because they germinate so rapidly they need eating immediately or the root radicles will become tough and flavour will deteriorate, since there is more nutrition in the shoots before leaves and roots have developed very far. This is why I'm so insistent on starting only small batches of seed.

After four or five days you will be able to tip the jar of bean shoots out into a colander to select a portion of the most forward for salad, returning the less developed sprouts to the jar to grow on for another day or two. Mung bean shoots are good with any mixture of salad stuffs, but especially with finely grated carrot, shredded Brussels sprouts or savoy, thinly sliced onion or leek, and the leaf salads that can be produced under protection in late winter and early spring.

101

Adzuki Beans

Adzuki beans with their red seed coats are as easy to grow and need similar treatment. A second method with either bean is to grow in a tray lined with towelling or several layers of kitchen paper roll. A small plastic seed tray is just the job. For this method of growing soak the seed in water for 24 hours, then move them onto the towelling or kitchen paper in the tray, which should have been thoroughly moistened.

Place the tray in a large polythene bag that has been pricked with a few tiny holes so that it is not airtight, and stand in a warm dark cupboard, or wrap in newspaper and stand on an open shelf. Water the beans two or three times a day, but don't allow them to become too wet and warm, or they will go mouldy. Harvest the sprouts at $1\frac{1}{2}$-2 ins long by pulling up as many as you need. By then, they should be plump and white with pale green leaves or, if you prefer a greener sample, this can be achieved by standing the tray in part light for the final day. Wash and serve as for bean shoots grown in a jam jar. Adzuki bean shoots are crisp with a sweet nutty flavour and are best used when a little shorter than mung sprouts.

Alphatoco Bean

The *alphatoco bean* sprout is produced in just the same way and has a crisper texture and sweeter flavour than the mung bean. It is rich in minerals and vitamins, but not so often seen as the other two bean sprouts.

Alfalfa

Alfalfa seeds are much smaller than those of the beans and should only be attempted by the jam jar method. Because of their size I find double gauze or muslin tops are needed to make sure that no seeds slip through the mesh during the twice daily rinsing. Be very sparing with seeds, for the volume builds up at a fantastic pace once growth begins. If you do make the mistake of growing too many at once you are wasting seeds – like a friend of mine who tipped the whole packet into a jar at her first try at growing. After a couple of days she had to divide the fast expanding mass of shoots between two jars and next day had to divide both of those lots, until at the end of a

Figure 39: Alfalfa sprouts ready to eat

week she ended with a row of jam jars full of fine shoots. I'd advise starting with just a tablespoonful for your first attempt – ^{1}2 oz of seed will give about 6 ozs of salad sprouts.

Alfalfa takes longer to reach table size than the beans and it will probably be six or seven days before the first is ready. Shoots have a delicious green pea flavour and are superb for sandwich fillings, for mixing into or garnishing a salad, or for serving like mustard and cress in piles on a platter of different salad items. Because growth is slower than for beans, alfalfa stays at its peak for longer, but I've found it is more inclined to damp off and go mouldy if you forget to rinse or leave too wet for too long. If you prefer green shoots keep your alfalfa jar on an open shelf or move to the kitchen windowsill after the first four or five days.

Fenugreek

Fenugreek is another smallish seed to grow by the jam jar method. Sprouts are best allowed to turn green before serving, have a spicy, curry-like flavour, and are rich in iron, protein and vitamin A. ^{1}2 oz of seed will yield about 4 ozs of sprouts, usually in five to seven days.

Mixed Seeds

You can buy packets of mixed seeds for sprouting, but I'm not keen on them because the different seeds need slightly different treatment and as some take much longer to develop than others you can seldom serve them mixed. With a jar grown from mixed seeds I've found that I had first to serve out the bean shoots, then the fenugreek and at the end some of the smallest seeds were wasted because they hadn't been able to compete with the bigger beans for moisture in the vital early stages.

Other Seeds

I think we are sure to see more and more types of seed offered for sprouting, because there are a whole variety of suitable things to experiment with. You might like to try your luck with lentils grown by the jam jar method: use whole lentils and they should be ready in five days. Sunflower seeds, perhaps from a giant bloom in one of your flower borders last summer, can be sprouted in about a week. They must be eaten when little more than $\frac{1}{2}$ in long, or flavour may become to strong.

Mustard and Cress

Mustard and cress need similar treatment to the other sprouting seeds, except that we grow them on until the seed leaves are fully expanded and don't eat the roots. Cress is slower growing and so you need to start this four or five days ahead of mustard if you want to harvest them together. I imagine that's the main reason why I never see cress in the shops these days, for time is precious in the economics of modern commercial growing. Come to that, you seldom see mustard, for what the supermarkets sell as salad cress is truly salad rape, preferred to mustard by the growers because rape grows more evenly, has greener leaves and is said to have a better flavour. Punnets are available all year round and so long as you buy only fresh samples are quite a good salad purchase.

But, why buy, when the real mustard and cress is so easy to grow and you need so very little space to produce your own? For cold weather production all you need is a kitchen windowsill where the temperature is unlikely to drop below 50°F (10°C), some kitchen paper roll and some shallow plastic dishes. Place a layer of the kitchen paper on a dish and moisten thoroughly, then broadcast cress seeds over the surface, repeating the process with mustard on another dish

four days later. Keep the sown trays in a warm dark place –
perhaps in the airing cupboard – until seeds have germinated
and shoots are an inch or so high.

Move the dishes to the windowsill to grow on until the seed
leaves have developed nicely and your crop will be ready to
harvest with the kitchen scissors or a sharp knife. During the
process you'll need to check the dishes a couple of times a day
to make sure that the paper lining and seeds stay moist, and
after the dishes are placed by the window you'll need to turn
them round each day to prevent one-sided growth. Shoots are
ideally 2 ins long at cutting time and can simply be rinsed in
cold water (you may have to rinse away a few seed coats),
drained and served. Use mustard and cress as an individual
salad stuff, mixed with leaf salads and other sprouting seeds,
as a garnish for any mixed salad, or as a sandwich filling.

Once warmer weather and early spring comes mustard and
cress can be produced easily in a cold greenhouse and I've
found that an early March showing, with others in fortnightly
succession, gives very welcome salads before many of the
lettuces are ready to cut. From mid-April I grow in the open,

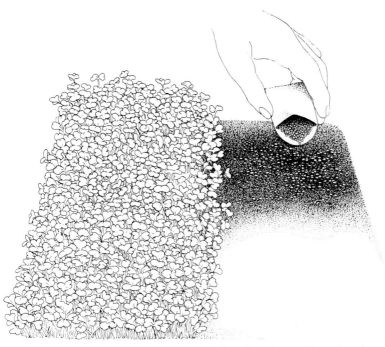

Figure 40: Sowing mustard seed on soil surface in small patch, with
some mustard and cress ready to harvest

but I tend only to sow in the warm months when I see that there is likely to be a gap in production of lettuce or some other shortage of salad stuffs.

In the greenhouse you can grow in trays lined with kitchen paper as indoors, or filled with peat or potting compost, but my method is to grow in the greenhouse border. I prepare a seed bed with a very fine tilth, rake this level and firm down the surface of the soil, allocating just the right size piece of ground to fit an upturned Dutch tomato tray used as a cover with the corner uprights pushed down into the soil. Of course, the site can be suited to whatever cover you have handy! Seed is broadcast thickly over the site, pressed into the soil surface with the flat of my hand and then I water the patch with a fine rose on the can – a coarse rose may allow water to dislodge the seed so you end up with it in heaps.

After this the cover goes on and apart from daily checking to see if more water is needed it stays on until the seedlings have germinated and are at least 1 in high – as indoors, cress will have been sown four days before the mustard and will probably want uncovering a day earlier. The uncovered seedlings are grown on for a few days until the seed leaves have expanded fully and turned green and then the double crop is ready to cut with scissors or knife. How long this takes to produce depends on the weather, but it is usually between 10 and 20 days.

In the open garden exactly the same technique is followed. Somtimes I'll use a larger cover and I've found that large baking tins no longer needed in the kitchen serve admirably. But, it is not wise to try and grow too much mustard and cress at one time, for in warm weather the seedlings soon develop too far forward for top quality table use. That's specially so with mustard, for few people like it after the rough and hot true leaves have started to appear.

Whether you are growing inside or out, the secret of success with this easy double crop is to make sure there is ample moisture for speedy growth, for we want succulent seed leaves and stems and not slowly-grown tough little sprouts.

Such a good salad and so easy to grow in a limited space, I can't imagine why so many people rely on the shops for salad rape when they could be enjoying real home-grown mustard and cress. If, like me, you want to produce steadily over some months, it is more economical to buy the ¼ lb (120 g) packet: small packets don't go far and cost proportionately far more.

Looking to the future, I'm convinced we are going to see an

expanding range of seeds recommended for sprouting and more emphasis placed on the vast fund of health-giving goodness that is to be found in a newly-germinated shoot. With building land so precious, gardens are tending to shrink, but all of us, even those who live in high-rise flats, can produce our own sprouting seeds for home-grown salads.

CHAPTER 14

Blanched Spring Stems

Seakale

Blanched seakale is delicious served raw in salads, but if you want to serve the stems you will have to grow at home, for you are most unlikely to find them at any greengrocers. Seldom seen in gardens today, this perennial vegetable could be thought too space-consuming for a small plot, but I believe it's a luxury worthy of a bit of land however precious. Like chicory, it is one of those crops that gardeners at big houses used to lift and force under the staging in their hot houses, but it's far easier to force *in situ* – though, of course, that will mean a rather later crop.

Historical Background

Seakale is a wild plant of our seashores and I've seen many a clump growing on the beach near Dungeness power station in Kent. In summer there are handsome blue-green, kale-like leaves that I've found good for foliage in larger flower arrangements and, if allowed to do so, the plants will produce a mass of tiny white cabbage-style flowers that have a honey scent. So, you see, seakale is a decorative plant through those warm months when garden display is of prime importance, as well as being productive in the lean salad weeks of early spring.

My introduction to seakale was in the garden of an old Kentish farmhouse whose owner didn't go to a great deal of trouble, yet was able to cut masses of pale succulent stems early in spring. The permanent bed at the end of his vegetable plot was fed generously and in autumn given a thick blanket of fallen leaves swept from lawn and paths. Around New Year the plants were covered with a series of upturned wooden boxes surrounded by more leaves and when he could obtain it some strawy manure, and by mid-March the first tender forced stems were ready to cut with a sharp knife. Some were cooked, but his wife believed they were best raw and served them regularly with such salad stuffs as finely grated carrot, sliced onion and shredded Brussels sprouts or cabbage.

Growing Your Own Seakale

The quickest way to start a bed is from pieces of root but, as they are almost impossible to buy – unless you know someone with a thriving clump – you'll probably need to raise plants from seed. 'Lily White' is a good variety obtainable from several firms, though not listed in many seed catalogues. Sow in the open in March or April on good soil, spacing the big seeds at least 6 ins apart to give room for each to make a sturdy plant for moving to the permanent bed next spring.

The site for this should be open and sunny on well-drained soil that's not deficient in lime and has been well supplied with organic matter. Sandy soils suit seakale well. The plant will stay in one place for some years and in the autumn before planting prepare the bed by double-digging and working in a bucketful of rotted manure or garden compost to every square yard. During winter apply lime if you are on land that's at all acid. Towards the end of March rake in a dressing of 4 ozs of general fertiliser to the square yard and a week or so later plant the crowns with tops 2 ins below soil level and 15 ins apart – if more than one row is grown, allow at least 18 ins between.

Water well in the coming weeks and in May mulch the new bed with more well rotted manure or garden compost and then in June give a dressing of 1 oz per sq yd of agricultural salt, something beloved by this seashore plant. If you are near the coast, or have space in the boot of the car on trips to the sea, there's nothing seakale likes better than a good mulch of seaweed. Don't let any plants run up to seed that first summer, for all their energy should go into building up strong clumps. The plants won't need the whole bed at first and so you can inter-plant with a catch crop of ridge cucumbers, lettuces, or salad onions and radishes.

As I've already said, the easiest way to force seakale is by covering the plants in their bed in January with upturned pots or boxes and you can still obtain special pots made for the job, though that's not the economic way of covering! All you need is a cover that will exclude all light and allow shoots to grow to 6-8 ins long before being cut. Obviously, the thicker the surrounding blanket of straw, leaves and manure the quicker

Figure 41: Seakale forced *in situ* under upturned boxes, with one removed to show stalks ready for cutting

your crop will come on, but in the first year it's wisest to force only very gently so that the plants can go on building up their strength.

Stop cutting blanched stems at the end of April, rake or very gently fork in a dressing of 3 ozs of general fertiliser to every sq yd and in a fortnight or so add a mulch of more well-rotted organic matter.

To force indoors, lift some of the crowns in autumn after leaves have died down naturally, trim off side roots, saving these for planting in spring, to give roots cut back to about 6 ins. Place these in large pots or boxes filled with John Innes potting compost No. 3, or a mixture of soil, leafmould and peat, covered with upturned pots or boxes of like size and stand in a dark place where the temperature is not likely to fall below 10°C (50°F). A cupboard under the stairs or a cellar will do well. Water the containers every ten days or so and, after about six weeks, you should be able to start cutting the first long slim stems that look a bit like sticks of celery and have a lovely nutty flavour.

To keep up a succession, lift and pot up more crowns in December and January, then follow on with seakale forced *in situ*. When selecting crowns for forcing take care that only healthy roots are chosen, for disease spreads rapidly in dark and warm places.

Those side roots cut off from lifted crowns should give some root cuttings of pencil thickness – 3-6 ins long. Cut them straight across at the top end nearest the main root and with a sloping cut at the bottom, and tie into bundles to store top end uppermost in sand or soil in a cold frame through winter. By late March they should be making buds at the top and you can rub off all but one big bud to each cutting, then plant as for making a new bed with root straight down and bud an inch below soil level. Do this every year and you are gradually replacing the bed as oldest crowns are lifted, forced and then thrown out as done for.

Serve forced seakale stems soon after cutting while crisp and succulent, chopping them to mix into almost any blend of crunchy winter and spring salad ingredients. When a few clumps are in full production you'll be surprised how many stems they yield and what a super standby these prove for salads at the leanest time of year.

Growing Your Own Salsify and Scorzonera

Salsify and Scorzonera

There are two other unusual vegetables which can be grown for blanched spring stems for salads, though both are more often grown as root crops. One of them is the *salsify*, known as the vegetable oyster because the white roots are supposed to have an oyster-like flavour. It's one of the Continental crops little grown in this country, but is listed in most seed catalogues. The other plant is *scorzonera*, known as viper's grass in Spain and once used as a medicinal herb to relieve snake bites and as a cure for indigestion. You'll often find the two grouped together because they need similar treatment both in the garden and in the kitchen.

Production of roots that look like the pictures in the catalogues isn't easy unless you have the deep, rich, light and stone-free soil the plants like, but even when roots have proved a disappointment you should still be able to harvest a good crop of the blanched stems that are commonly referred to as 'chards'. Chief difference in appearance between these two roots is that salsify looks rather like a long white carrot, while scorzonera has ebony skins like a 'Black Spanish' winter radish.

Because roots grow long the plants need a good deeply-dug soil, but never make the mistake of growing them on land that has been recently manured or you will have forked roots of no use at all in the kitchen. Fit them into the same part of the rotation as carrots and other root crops, preparing the site by working soil down to a fine tilth and raking in a dressing of 2-3 ozs of general fertiliser to each sq yd.

Sow seed in April or May in ½ in-deep drills 1 ft apart with two or three seeds every 6 ins in readiness for thinning to one per station as soon as the seedlings are large enough to handle. During summer it's very important to hand weed around the plants, for their narrow leaves are not broad enough to smother weeds and working too close with a hoe may damage the developing roots and cause them to bleed. A mulch of old potting compost, peat or the contents of a twice-used growing bag will help keep down weeds and conserve moisture, but even with that you will need to water in dry spells.

Roots can be lifted from mid-October as needed in the kitchen, using a fork inserted to its full depth and taking great care not to spike the tender skins and cause bleeding. Although more often cooked, both salsify and scorzonera roots are excellent in winter salads if grated and sprinkled with lemon juice to prevent discolouring before serving. But, I think the plants' main use is for production of the blanched shoots in spring, and for this roots should be left in the ground all winter.

Cut leaves down to an inch from ground level in autumn and earth up the row with 6 ins of soil, or cover the plants with about 6 ins of dry leaves or straw – leaving this task until late winter if you wish. New spring foliage will push up through the covering to give blanched stems 5 or 6 ins long to serve in salads. Mix them with any blend of ingredients, either whole or broken up, perhaps letting the chards take the place of a forced chicon of shop chicory.

You can instead serve the leaves green, but the blanched foliage is generally considered to be of superior flavour.

112

Among varieties look out for 'Sandwich Island Mammoth' salsify and 'Russian Giant' or 'Large Black' scorzonera.

CHAPTER 15

Endive

The plants in the last chapter should be covered early in the year to hasten spring growth and give pale shoots of good table quality. Endive comes at the opposite end of the season and is fully grown before being covered to blanch the bitter leaves until they are creamy-green and sweet enough for salad eating.

Mrs Beeton regarded endive as one of the principal constituents of a winter salad and recommended arranging the leaves with surrounding rings of sliced cooked beetroot and hard-boiled eggs, with perhaps also chopped celery and mustard and cress. It is one of those luxury crops more popular in her day of large houses with large gardens and a large staff of gardeners who could supply vegetables that needed a fair amount of attention.

Endive is available in better-class greengrocers, mainly in autumn and winter, but tends to be rather costly. Unfortunately, a long journey from grower to shop and perhaps a spell in a brightly-lit window can result in poorly blanched heads that will not be nearly so good to eat as pale endive brought in from the garden. So, if you've tried shop leaves and thought them too bitter, do try growing your own and comparing the difference in quality.

Whether you buy or cut from the garden, use endive as soon as possible. Trim off outer damaged leaves and surplus root, wash and drain, separating the shoots, and serve with any blend of salad stuffs that would mix with lettuce.

Historical
Background

A plant that's believed to have originated in Egypt and was used as a salading by the Romans, endive has been grown in England since the sixteenth century. Basically there are two types, one with decorative curly leaves and the other a hardier kind with broad plain leaves that can follow on into winter. In our seed catalogues you will usually find them listed as 'Moss Curled' and 'Batavian Broad-leaved', but on the Continent more varieties are grown and the Dutch seed house of Bakker give more choice. Their range includes the new 'President', a yellow-heart endive with curly leaves that's resistant to cold; a 'Large Green Curled' with pink leaf ribs; and 'Avant Garde Winter' that's of robust quality and withstands bad weather conditions.

Growing Your Own Endive

Some people sow endive in succession from spring on, but sowings made before June are prone to bolt and I believe the value of the crop is as a follow on to summer salad stuffs. Because of that a late June sowing to give heads for cutting in October is the start to my season, with one or two more of the hardier type to extend the supply into early winter.

Don't be put off by the work involved in blanching, for in these days of inexpensive black plastic sheeting and plastic flower pots that's not a big problem. Of course, endive involves more care and attention than lettuce, but just compare prices in the shops and you will see that this is a luxury worth the effort.

Ideal land for the crop is fairly light and well-drained with manure or garden compost supplied during the winter. June sowings can follow early lettuce and July sowings the early peas and broad beans that enjoyed this recently-manured ground. Regular watering is the secret of growing successfully without plants running up to seed before their time and this almost certainly will mean watering during drier weather on a weekly basis. Unless land is very fertile a few doses of liquid fertiliser applied with the water will be beneficial.

Sow seed thinly in $\frac{1}{2}$ in-deep drills 1 ft apart, preferably with just a tiny pinch of seed every 9 or 12 ins so you can thin to one plant per station. Some say thinnings cannot be transplanted, as they will bolt, but when moved young and given ample moisture endive can be transplanted successfully.

The broad-leaved endive needs a bit more room than the curly so give that 12 ins between plants against 9 ins for 'Moss Curled' (known in France as 'Chicorees Frisees'). From this you will see that the plant is a relative of the chicory and in the early stages it's hard to differentiate from the 'Sugar Loaf' chicory that's sown around the same time.

115

Figure 42: Tying endive head with raffia and covering with upturned flower pot

About twelve weeks from sowing, when endive is fully grown, you can start the blanching process by tying the leaves together with raffia, taking care not to cut or bruise them. Do this on a dry day so that no moisture is trapped inside the plant. Complete the blanching by covering a few plants at a time – once pale they soon spoil and so you won't want the entire row ready for table at one time. The traditional method was to cover each plant with an inverted flower pot with a bit of crock across the drainage hole to exclude all light. Because ventilation is important to prevent risk of decay, the pot should be stood on two or three bits of crock so air can get in underneath.

Particularly with the later row sown at the end of July and intended for winter eating, covering with cloches from mid-October can be of great value to endive – again choose a dry day for covering. The cloched crop can be blanched by adding a second cover of black plastic sheeting over one short length of the row at a time and, should hard weather threaten, you can protect further with a blanket of straw or old newspaper.

Blanching usually takes about three weeks, but may take quite a bit less in warm weather early in autumn. It's wise to inspect plants regularly to ensure no rot has started – for once decay has set in you may as well scrap those plants and try again — and to see how blanching is progressing so that the first heads can be cut immediately they are ready. Slugs can be a bother with the covered plants and so you'll probably need to put down bait, well protected from domestic pets and wild birds.

All this may make endive sound an awful bother, but I've already said that I think it's a luxury worth some trouble. I do think too that this is more a crop for the housewife, who can give her plants a bit of attention most days than for the busy man who can only garden on Sundays. Let him grow the hard work crops like maincrop potatoes and leave his wife the fiddly ones that need a bit of loving care!

Having said that, I believe endive is one of those less usual salad stuffs to be grown by every gardener who wants to know how to produce a full range of crops. Serve up a platter of the delicately blanched leaves mixed with home-grown celery, sliced long beetroot from your own store, plus a garnish of land cress and other leaf salads and you can feel you have achieved success as a salad grower. That'll give far more satisfaction than could be gained from cutting a lettuce and a cucumber in the middle of summer.

CHAPTER 16

Sweet Peppers

If endive could be classed as a Victorian salad, sweet peppers are definitely twentieth century and it is only in the last few years that their value for eating raw has been realised. Come to that, it is only in recent years that they have been recognised as a crop everyone can grow.

Historical
Background

So many people want to grow sweet peppers these days that it is hard to realise that a generation ago they were seldom eaten in this country and a quite new addition to the pages of our seed lists. They were discovered in America in the sixteenth century by the Spanish explorers and have been grown widely in Spain and some surrounding areas for a long time but, though the seventeenth-century herbalist John Gerard is said to have introduced a hot chilli pepper, or as he called it a ginny pepper, to England, the plants didn't catch on here until British housewives of recent years started to enthuse over American and European cookery.

Although it is possible to grow sweet peppers in milder areas outside in a good year, I would not advise anyone to attempt growing them in the open garden, especially as these days most of us can provide some form of protection. The plants do very well in pots and are a decorative choice for growing in a conservatory, sun lounge or on a sunny windowsill, for the fruits are fascinating to watch as they develop and turn from green to yellow or red. The green peppers we mainly use are immature fruits and if left long enough on the plants would change colour.

Serving Sweet
Peppers

One fruit goes a long way when sliced raw for salads and so

Figure 43: Sweet pepper growing in flower pot on windowsill

you need not be very extravagant if you rely on the shops. Pay
a luxury price for one pepper and use it for several days to
titivate more mundane mixtures of inexpensive shredded
cabbage, grated carrot and sliced leek or onion in a winter
salad. I might add that this is a valuable addition to a healthy
diet, for peppers are exceptionally high in vitamin C whether
eaten in the unripe green state or when they've turned to
yellow or red.

The red is perhaps rather better for garnishing a mixed
salad, though in summer when tomatoes are plentiful the
green is perhaps of greatest value; while for maximum effect
you can top a salad with red, yellow and green pepper cut into
tiny pieces. Sweet peppers, whether from the shop or garden,
need no preparation for table apart for removing the stalk and
hard circle surrounding its base and taking out the seeds that
are too hard to enjoy.

Sweet Peppers

Growing Your Own Sweet Peppers

If you aim to grow at home you must start off in warmth, as a comparatively high temperature is needed to germinate pepper seeds. However, there's no need for a heated greenhouse, as you can manage well with an electric propagator or by standing pots of sown seeds on a windowsill above a warm radiator. As soon as seedlings are large enough to handle, prick them out into individual 3-ins pots of John Innes potting compost No. 1 or a soil-less equivalent to grow on in gentle heat. From a late March sowing on a warm windowsill, I've been very successful in producing plants to go out to a cold greenhouse or under cloches in early June – unless you have heat it is unwise to plant out before that.

You can plant directly into the greenhouse border, but growing on in 9-ins pots filled with John Innes potting compost No. 2, or in growing bags, is often more successful. Pinching out the growing tip of the plants at about 6 ins high encourages bushy development. During the growing season sweet peppers need similar treatment to tomatoes, but require more heat and a more humid atmosphere.

One friend of mine has a super tunnel house he designed and made himself from pieces of spare timber and a large heavy duty polythene sheet. He has partitioned off about a third of this with more polythene sheet and very fine plastic mesh so that there is a warmer more humid end for his cucumbers and peppers and a large area that is cooler and more airy for tomatoes. The house is sited in a sunny sheltered spot and with generous amounts of manure dug in during winter and water throughout summer he has some wonderful crops.

With pot-grown plants, in particular, watering must be regular and liquid feed will be needed also. Syringing the plants every day with water throughout the flowering period helps maintain a humid atmosphere and prevent trouble from red spider, which can be a problem with the crop.

If you aim to grow under cloches choose a sunny sheltered site on well-drained fertile land that was supplied with rotted manure or garden compost during winter. Before planting out rake in 2 ozs per sq yd of general fertiliser. Under cold glass no variety is likely to exceed 2 ft high, so you may be able to raise cloches so that they can stay in position all through the season. Water regularly and from the time that the fruits begin to swell apply liquid feed.

Wherever you've grown your peppers, it's wise to start

Figure 44: Young pepper plants being planted three to a growing bag

harvesting as soon as the first fruits are near to full size, for this will help the rest of the crop develop well. Later on you can allow some to stay on the plants until they are yellow or red, but as green peppers are just as good to eat it helps the yield and extends the season to start by using some of them.

Under cloches or in a border you need to allow 18 ins between most varieties and these are best put in at three to a growing bag, but a closer spacing of 14 ins is sufficient for a dwarf variety like the 10-ins high 'Triton' that produces dunce's cap-style peppers about 4 ins long and makes a showy pot plant to grow along with tuberous-rooted begonias and other ornamentals in a conservatory.

For main use I prefer the big blocky fruits of the size and shape favoured by the commercial growers and most often seen in the shops. There's a good selection of these to choose from and every season the seed catalogues include new varieties with mouth-watering descriptions. Given an Award of Merit by the Royal Horticultural Society and outstanding for earliness and yield in the RHS trials, the F_1 hybrid 'Early Prolific' is a good choice for greenhouse, or cloches. Another good hybrid that earned the same award and can be grown inside or under cloches is 'Canape'.

In time their fruits will turn to red, but the newer 'Goldstar' and 'Yellow Lantern' have big blocky fruits that start green and turn to bright gold when ripe. Use them for pots, growing bags or in the border inside, or under cloches in the open garden.

Sweet peppers are a crop you can grow even if you have no

open garden, for, as I've already said, they'll do well in pots or growing bags and can be grown from seed to maturity on a windowsill, in a sun lounge, or on a sunny balcony.

CHAPTER 17

Other Vegetables

Vegetables in this chapter are used mainly for hot meals, but occasionally make ingredients for interesting salads. Some of them can be served raw, while others are always better cooked first however you intend to present them on the table.

Asparagus

Asparagus is a luxury vegetable that's seldom served in salads, but whose cold cooked tips are rolled in cream cheese or ham and thin fingers of brown bread for cocktail snacks at parties. Use them also for garnishing late spring and early summer salads, or mixed with wedges of tomato on a bed of shredded lettuce with a topping of finely chopped parsley or other herbs. For salad eating you only want the choicest tips of the asparagus spears, but there is no need to waste the rest as the coarser parts are very good for making soup.

If you grow asparagus at home you find that spears tend to appear just two or three at a time and to collect enough for a good feed you must cut some and save them in a glass of water in a cool place until more are ready. But, for salads, just a couple of tips per person are sufficient and so it doesn't matter if the crop is sparse.

Perhaps it would be foolish to devote space in a tiny garden to this vegetable, but it is a luxury well worth including if you can find room for a traditional bed 5 ft wide that will take three rows of plants, or for the more modern long single row that is easier to manage. Whichever you choose, you must plant on deeply dug soil that has been well supplied with organic matter before the plants go in during April and must wait two years before the first harvest. Asparagus is a long-term investment and, once a bed is established, it will go on for a generation with only routine care.

Other Vegetables

Beans

Almost every gardener grows *beans* of one kind or another and the broad, dwarf and runner varieties can all be used in salads. You do find recipes incorporating various dried beans, but I've purposely avoided them because there has been concern over the health risk they may bring when eaten in this way. All my salad beans are home-grown and green, and are always cooked first, though you may like to try tiny broad beans raw.

At the age they find their way to the shops or are picked by many gardeners *broad beans* are too tough for salads, but if you are grower and cook, or have access to the row, you can gather pods while the beans inside are no bigger across than a new penny piece. You'll find these young beans are very good cooked and served cold in salads.

You can sow the hardier *longpod* type in November, but that's rather a gamble with the weather and so I prefer to rely on a first sowing under cloches in January or February or, should weather then be hard, to sow in a Dutch tomato tray of potting compost in the greenhouse to transplant outside towards the end of March. The 'Broad Windsor'-type can be sown as a follow on, but I think the most valuable broad beans are the early ones ready to eat before the end of June and cleared from the garden in time for July salad sowings.

Dwarf beans started under cloches in April should come in after the broad beans and before the runners and though grown mainly for cooking are delicious when served cold in salads. For this try a stringless green variety like 'Sprite' or 'Tendergreen' picked while young.

Runner beans are such a popular summer crop, but unfortunately too many gardeners sow one row in mid-May and end up with a glut over a few weeks. A far better way is to stagger the sowing by putting in one-third of the row under cloches in April or at the same time in pots in the greenhouse to transplant outside when frost risk is past, then sow more in mid-May, and finally put in the rest of the row in early June. That way, given fertile soil and ample water in dry spells, you should be able to gather fresh green beans from July to the end of October.

Peas

Green *peas* are one of most people's favourite summer

vegetables and are delicious in salads whether cooked or served raw straight from the pods. To be fully enjoyed though they must be young and tender with no hint of hard skins and floury middles. Given fertile soil they are not difficult to grow, but are attacked by more enemies than most vegetables: from mice that eat the seeds before they germinate, to birds that peck off the emerging shoots and pea moths whose eggs hatch out to become the maggots we all hate to find in the pods. Despite some problem in controlling pests and diseases, and perhaps because of it, there's an enormous satisfaction in being able to gather a basket of peas from your own garden and, once you've eaten them straight from the row, the peas from the shops will never seem so good again.

For eating raw gather a few pods two or three days before the peas are ready to pick and spoil yourself with the tenderest, sweetest peas you've ever tried. You could cook them for a salad, but at that age it's a sin to eat them any way but raw directly after shelling.

Nowadays most people grow dwarf varieties but, given plastic pea and bean netting for support, it's not difficult to grow a taller heavier cropping variety like the 5 ft plus 'Alderman'. Though not quite so early as the hardy round-seeded peas that can be sown from November to January, the marrowfats are of superior eating quality and so I prefer to wait for them. Among the first of those wrinkled-seeded varieties is the 18 ins-high 'Hurst Beagle' that can be started under cloches and for a maincrop it's hard to better the 30 ins-high 'Hurst Green Shaft'. French cooks favour the small and very sweet 'Petit Pois'-type peas which can be sown from March to June and are good for freezing as well as using fresh – 'Waverex' is a good variety.

Courgettes

Few people would want to eat raw marrow: far better is sliced raw *courgette* – baby marrow cut at 4-5 ins long before the seeds have begun to grow out and harden You can use the green varieties, but for salad eating I prefer 'Golden Zucchini' and 'Goldrush' whose small fruits cut into thin slices add a bright yellow to the salad bowl.

You can grow marrows and courgettes completely in the open, sowing seed in mid-May, but I believe you do far better to start the seeds in 3-ins pots in a cold greenhouse in late April to give plants to put out at the end of May. Plant on land

125

generously supplied with organic matter in winter or on specially prepared stations (separate sites for each plant, approximately 3 ft apart).

Add a mulch of lawn mowings to help keep the roots cool and moist, be generous with water and give occasional liquid feed, and you'll have a bumper crop over many weeks.

Spinach

Spinach is a crop to grow mainly for cooking, but the tender young leaves are very good torn up and served with a mixture of leaf and other salads.

This crop is most valuable in spring when over-wintered plants begin to make new growth, and will come earliest if the row is given a fillip of nitrate of soda or some other quick-acting fertiliser in late February, plus the protection of cloches. 'Sigmaleaf' is a good winter hardy variety to sow in late July on land vacant because early summer crops have been cleared. Sown thinly and then gradually thinned to 6 ins apart, this will give small leaves for use raw from August on and should ideally be covered with cloches in October or November to allow some picking through winter. The same variety can be sown in March for summer eating and will again give thinnings whose small leaves are good raw.

Spinach beet is very easy to grow and usually I sow in late May to give a row for picking through summer and autumn and again in spring. For salad use the first spring leaves are the most valuable, but do try the new leaves that are just a bit less developed than those we normally gather for cooking.

Swiss chard, known too as seakale beet, is grown in the same way as spinach beet. Its thick white midribs are sometimes cooked as a substitute for seakale, while the leaf blade is cooked like spinach.

Turnips

Most of us associate *turnips* with hot meals and I never feel a stew seems complete without a few slices from one of these tasty and quickly-grown roots. I don't think I would ever use a large older turnip raw, but when I have a row of tender young white turnips of golf ball size they are sliced to go in salads just like radishes. Never sow very many turnips at one time, for they soon pass the peak of perfection, but instead sow small amounts of seed every month from March to August. 'Snowball' has long been my favourite, with round pure white roots that are very sweet and mild when pulled young. For summer they must have soil that will never be allowed to dry out and given this will be ready in less than two months from sowing.

Swedes

Swedes need a far longer season and are best sown at the end of May to pull for eating from the end of October to March. Again, they must have soil that retains moisture through the hot months and you must sow them very, very thinly as roots are best thinned to 9 ins apart – the best roots for table are those of at least 6 ins across! Most swedes will be used for hot winter meals, but do try a bit of the root thinly sliced, diced or grated and mixed raw in a blend of other crunchy vegetables.

Kohlrabi

Kohlrabi is a relative of the turnip that's not widely grown, through you'll find it listed in most vegetable seed catalogues. The swollen root-like stems have a distinctive flavour and can be cooked like turnip or sliced raw in salads. The crop needs a fertile, well-drained soil and must be given ample food and water so there is growth without check, or the edible part may be tough and unenjoyable. Sow from April to July to harvest about 12 weeks later on when the 'roots' are around tennis ball size.

Parsnips

Parsnips are a crop that I regard as a winter standby for cooking, but sometimes part of a root will be grated in salads with maincrop carrots, shredded savoy and sliced leek. Old-fashioned gardeners sowed the seed in late February and often produced large roots affected by canker, but modern practice is to sow seed in late March or early April and to thin to no more than 4 ins to give smaller roots seldom troubled by the complaint. Newer dumpy varieties like 'Avonresister' and 'White Gem' are, I believe, of far superior table quality to the older, longer parsnips.

Sweet Corn

Sweet corn is a comparatively recent addition to our list of vegetables for growing at home, but with the introduction of modern hybrid forms that will develop cobs in the few short months of our variable English summer, this is becoming increasingly popular with the home gardener. Most cobs are cut when young and tender and boiled to eat hot with melted butter or in some other recipe, but the nutritious young corn stripped from the cob makes a good addition to summer salads. Canned or frozen corn can be used in the same way at other seasons.

A half-hardy annual, sweet corn must be started inside, but is easy to raise from seed and if sown in individual 3-ins pots in April will give plants to go out in late May. Given a fertile soil, plenty of food and water, an F_1 hybrid like 'Sundance' will give a good crop of 7-ins long cobs. They are ready to harvest when a grain of corn pressed with a fingernail exudes a creamy liquid. Never cook for too long, as this leads to tough kernels. Corn is wind pollinated and so is better planted in a block with 12 to 15 ins between plants than in a long row.

Finnochio (Fennel)

My last suggestion is another half-hardy, the 'Florence' fennel, or *finnochio*, more often bought from the shops, but

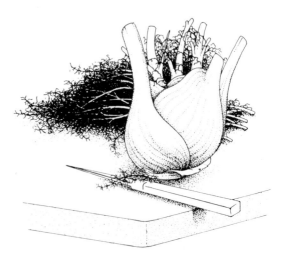

Figure 45: Head of 'Florence' fennel being trimmed during preparation for eating

128

sometimes grown at home. It is a relative of our herb the common fennel, with a bulb-like swollen leaf base that's regarded as a luxury vegetable with an aniseed flavour. An Italian plant that thrives in the warm Mediterranean climate, this needs a warm, well-drained soil well fed with organic matter. The new variety 'Zefa Fino' is particularly recommended for early maturity and resistance to bolting. Seed can be sown inside for transplanting or direct into the open garden in April. When the leaf bases start to swell plants must be earthed up to give the plump blanched finnochio we need for the kitchen.

You can use the leaves finely chopped in place of common fennel to add an aromatic flavour to summer salads – this is specially good with cucumber or a mixed green salad – but use sparingly as the Italian fennel is stronger than ours. Prepare the 'bulb' by trimming away the leafy top of the stems and saving leaves for garnishing, then trim off the root base and wash thoroughly. Cut the finnochio in half lengthwise and across into thin slices to serve raw in salads.

CHAPTER 18

Herbs

In previous chapters I have included some of the herbs that I use most often in salads, but there are many more of these aromatic plants that can be used to make our salads more exciting. I will now go through some more of them – in alphabetical order.

Angelica

Angelica is a tall handsome plant usually grown as a biennial and happiest on deep rather moist soil in part shade – it's a near relative of our wild angelica. With big divided leaves and

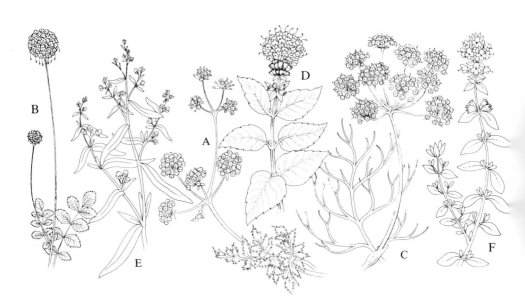

Figure 46: Assortment of sprigs of herbs: (A) chervil, (B) salad burnet, (C) dill, (D) mint, (E) French tarragon, (F) thyme

great branching plants topped by umbels of greenish flowers, you will find that an angelica plant can make a good focal point at the back of a border.

The main culinary use is to give candied stems for cake decorating, but you may like to try tiny amounts of the fresh green leaves of early summer chopped and sprinkled over the salad bowl, or small pieces of the peeled raw stem mixed in with other ingredients.

Anise

Anise is a little sun-loving annual whose seeds are well known for giving aniseed flavouring. If you grow the herb from a sowing on a light well-drained soil in April, you can sprinkle a few of the finely chopped leaves over a summer salad. Plants will grow to around 18 ins with deeply-cut, green leaves and loose flat clusters of yellow-white flowers in July; but in this country seed will only ripen after a good summer.

(Lemon) Balm

Such an easy perennial to grow, *lemon balm* has been a favourite for centuries with hive owners because bees are so fond of the insignificant tubular, white summer flowers. Just one plant will make a good-sized clump on most soils and two or three of the heart-shaped leaves chopped and sprinkled over the salad bowl will impart a delicious lemony tang. Propagation is by root division and you can plant at any time in the dormant season – the balm won't object to a bit of shade.

(Sweet) Basil

Best treated in this country as a half-hardy annual, *sweet basil* needs a warm sheltered site on well-drained fertile soil. Seed should be sown in mid-April inside to give plants to go out in late May and best results are obtained if seedlings are pricked out into individual pots to minimise root disturbance. Through summer plants will benefit from regular watering in dry spells to encourage succulent leaves, and flower spikes should be pinched out to encourage a bushy habit and continuous growth. Basil makes a good pot plant for the greenhouse in

131

summer and in cold districts that's the best way to treat the herb. The young clove-scented leaves are specially good when shredded over a tomato salad, or any salad with tomato as a major ingredient.

Borage

An easy hardy annual, *borage* will often self-seed and my best plants usually seem to appear in this way, though I've never found the herb a nuisance with the habit. Sow seed in April where intended to flower, choosing a sunny site on almost any well-drained soil. Plants grow rapidly and by June you'll have rough hairy young leaves to gather and chop to add a cool cucumber taste to salads. The bright blue flowers, that show the plant is a relative of the forget-me-not, are very good for sprinkling over a salad as a final garnish just before the bowl goes on the table.

Burnet

Salad *burnet* is a perennial plant of the chalk downs that sheep love to graze over. It has been planted in herb gardens since Roman times and will thrive on an ordinary well-drained soil in sun or part shade, sometimes being used to fill cracks between paving because of the lovely scent given off when leaves are bruised as people walk over the path.

Plants can be raised from seed sown in a frame in April and planted out 10 ins apart when large enough to handle, but propagation is more often by root division and you may prefer to buy plants. The pinnate leaves are made up of four to twelve pairs of bright-green, oval toothed leaflets which give off an aroma of cucumber when bruised. They are very good chopped in salads and especially so in winter and spring when green leaves are not so plentiful. In summer it is wise to cut off flowering stems to encourage formation of the new leaves that are the best to eat.

Caraway

Caraway is a biennial of the parsley family that is best known as an ingredient of seed cakes. Choose a sunny open site on well-drained land and sow in July and August to give white flowers followed by seeds the next summer. You can sow in a row, but a patch of thinly broadcast seed thinned to 8 ins each way in the herb plot looks more attractive. For salads, chop the young leaves finely and sprinkle sparingly over the bowl as a garnish. If you are uninterested in seeds, you can sow in spring to provide leaves only, scrapping the plants as soon as the later sowings have produced foliage large enough to harvest.

Chervil

I included *chervil* among leaf salads and so all I'll say now is that this is one of the plants used in the fines herbes beloved by French cooks. The mixture consists of equal parts of finely chopped chervil, chives, parsley and tarragon and they are all plants I believe essential in the salad lover's herb plot. With protection through the cold months and regular small sowings from March to September, it's not difficult to provide fresh chervil all year round.

Chives

Also needed for fines herbes, *chives* were included in the chapter on the onion family and are an absolute must for anyone who makes a lot of salads. Believed to have more culinary uses than any other herb, they have been grown in cottage gardens since earliest times and are decorative enough to go in a flower border. Easy to grow in pots and troughs they can be potted up to grow on in the greenhouse or on a windowsill so there's a supply through the dormant season.

Costmary

Costmary, sometimes called alecost, is a perennial of the chrysanthemum family that was grown in almost every sixteenth-century herb garden but is not much seen today. Probably that was because the plant was used to flavour ale in the days before hops were introduced to this country. Propagation of this easy perennial is by root division, and plants will grow to 2 ft or more high with grey-green leaves that have a slightly bitter mint taste and are usually available in winter after mint has died down to the ground. When grown in full sun the plants produce clusters of tansy-like small yellow button blooms. The leaves are most often used as an ingredient of potpourri, but a few finely chopped are well worth trying in a salad.

Dill

Dill is an aromatic hardy annual that's rather like a miniature fennel and whose seeds were made into the dill water that was so often used in the past to soothe unhappy babies. One of the many Mediterranean herbs thought to have been brought to Britain by the Romans, this will make plants a couple of feet high with feathery leaves and umbels of yellow bloom.

Sow outdoors in April or May in a sunny spot where drainage is good and thin to 1 ft apart. Use the decorative leaves to chop and sprinkle over the salad bowl as a garnish and to impart a slightly bitter aniseed-like flavour. Dill is specially good with cucumber and beetroot. After flowering come the seeds so famous for dill water and they must be gathered immediately they are ripe, or they will fall to the ground. The best way is to pull up the plants or cut them off at ground level as the main flowerheads become brown. Tie plants in bunches and hang upside down in a sunny airy place to finish ripening with a cloth underneath to catch the falling seeds. Use the seeds whole or ground to add a distinctive flavour to autumn and winter salads.

(Common) Fennel

Like a larger version of dill, the *common fennel* has feathery leaves that are widely used in sauces to serve with fish. These same pretty leaves are very good for chopping to sprinkle over summer salads either on their own or blended with parsley and other herbs, being particularly good with cucumber or a green salad. An attractive perennial that grows wild in some places, usually near the seaside, fennel may reach 5 ft high and is a branching plant topped by umbels of yellowish-green flowers followed by seeds used in savoury dishes and to sprinkle over bread, cakes and biscuits. The plant likes a sunny position, preferably on well-drained soil that is also moisture-retentive, and is good-looking enough to grow in a flower border.

The herb is quite easy to raise from seed sown in the open in a sunny position in April or May and will self-seed, though for maximum leaf production it may be wisest to cut growth to the base at intervals through summer to prevent flowering and encourage lots of fresh foliage.

Hyssop

Hyssop is a shrubby perennial herb from the Mediterranean regions with narrow, aromatic evergreen foliage and spikes of tubular flowers in summer that are usually deep-blue but may be pink or white. This needs a sunny site and good drainage and though you can grow from seed is more often propagated from 2-ins cuttings taken from sideshoots in April or May. The plant grows to between 1-2 ft and will live for several years, proving a great favourite with honey bees. Being evergreen, hyssop is a herb we can use in salads all year and the chopped leaves add a sharp tang that's rather like a bitter mint. In summer you can also sprinkle a few flowers over the salad bowl as a garnish.

Lovage

Lovage is a perennial, believed to have been brought here by the Romans, with a scent and taste rather like strong celery. In appearance it is rather like a giant cow parsley, sometimes reaching 8 ft high with glossy dark-green divided leaves and umbels of small yellowish-green flowers that may be 6 ins across and are followed by brown seeds. Easily raised from seed, but often propagated by root division, lovage does well in most soils but is happiest on a deep moist loam in sun or part shade. One or two plants will be enough to supply a family. Much used medicinally in olden days, the herb has been widely used to add a celery flavour to cooked dishes when that vegetable was out of season. The young and tender leaves are good shredded in salads and removing flower stems will help encourage new foliage to come.

(Sweet or Knotted) Marjoram

A cousin of the wild marjoram that's so colourful along the roadsides on our chalk downs, the *sweet* or *knotted marjoram* is an annual herb native to warmer climes that is best treated as a half-hardy in England. It has a milder more pleasant flavour than our wild plant and will make a small upright bush a foot or more high with small pale lilac, pink or white flowers and greyish leaves. You can sow seed in the open in late May, but it is better to sow under cold glass in March to give plants to go outside 6-10 ins apart in May. A supply can be maintained through winter if some plants from the open garden are potted up to grow on in a frost-free greenhouse from late September on. Leaves gathered fresh from the plant have many uses in the kitchen and finely chopped are particularly good sprinkled over tomato salads.

(Spear)mint

Among the various different types of mint, *spearmint,* is the one most widely used in the kitchen. Most cooks use sprigs to cook with new potatoes and peas and to make into mint sauce to accompany roast lamb, but surprisingly few people add leaves to their salads. Such an easy perennial to grow, spearmint is too often relegated to an old corner by the compost heap, but I like a clump close to the back door so I can pop out from the kitchen to gather a few leaves whenever they are needed in a recipe.

Given a chance, the running roots will commandeer far more than their share of the garden, but that problem can be overcome if mint roots are planted in a bottomless bucket or tub sunk rim deep in the soil. Whether grown in sun or part shade, this herb likes a moisture-retentive soil and so the site should be well dug and generously fed with rotted organic matter before planting, while watering in dry spells and a spring mulch of garden compost will help maintain quality. It is best to replant every three or four years on a new site or after the existing one has been dug over and well nourished with rotted manure or garden compost. To keep up production through the dormant season, plant a few roots in a box of potting compost in early October to grow on in the greenhouse.

Nasturtium

More often listed among flowers than herbs, the *nasturtium* is a very easy hardy annual that came to us in the seventeenth century from South America and was used there as a food plant by the natives, thus acquiring the old common name of

Indian cress. Save the modern dwarf compact varieties for edgings and the double 'Gleam' hybrids for hanging baskets and use the old climbing single nasturtiums to cover rapidly netting, a trellis or a hedge for summer colour and screening. Their leaves will be borne most abundantly in a cooler richer soil and though I agree that this annual is better in sunny dryish places when flowers are wanted, I like to poke in a few seeds in a more fertile place to encourage lush leaf production. Tear up the freshly gathered leaves and use sparingly to add an excitingly different spicy flavour to green salads through summer and until sharp frosts come in autumn. Unless winter is very hard, you will almost certainly find a few self-sown seedling nasturtiums coming up in spring and so one packet should keep you supplied for some years.

Parsley

Parsley went into the leaf salad chapter because I use it that way rather than as a garnish, but it is one of the most nutritious herbs we have and deserves another mention here. Such a valuable plant needs treating well and that means a site on fertile moisture-retentive soil, watering through dry spells and giving some liquid feed a few times in summer to keep up steady production of new leaves. The youngest newest foliage is the best for eating raw and regular picking also helps encourage new growth. Covering the row with cloches, or lifting some plants to grow in pots in the greenhouse, or on a windowsill, will keep up a supply through the cold months.

The herb's popularity as a garnish is partly because the curly green foliage looks so good, but largely because the leaves retain their crisp green appearance for a long time after harvesting. That may be so, but for salads do use only leaves straight from the plant, for they are much nicer and much more nourishing. It is said that chewing parsley will take away the smell of onion and garlic from the breath – a good reason for adding a generous topping of chopped leaves to salads containing members of the onion family. You may prefer a sharp knife and a chopping board for larger quantities, but I find the kitchen scissors ideal for cutting parsley and other herbs and, with these held over the salad bowl or platter, can sprinkle as I cut.

Savory

There are two types of *savory*, one an annual for summer and the other an evergreen perennial to use through winter. Sow the milder summer savory in shallow drills in April in a fertile well-drained soil in a sunny part of the garden and, when seedlings are large enough to handle, thin to 9 ins each way. They will make small leafy bushes to give shoots for cutting from midsummer until autumn frosts come. A sowing in a pan in September can be pricked out into individual 3-ins pots of potting compost to grow on in a cool greenhouse, or on a windowsill, to give summer savory through winter. Leaves have a distinctive and very pleasant flavour and are best used sparingly. The herb has long been traditional with broad beans and used to be grown to cook with veal and venison, but I think you'll find a few leaves good in a salad.

Winter savory is a sub-shrubby perennial that likes a sunny dryish spot, but may not last long on more fertile ground. Plant out roots in spring, dividing older plants then if they are beginning to show signs of becoming over-large and straggly. Similar in appearance to its summer cousin, this has a slightly more spreading habit and larger pale-lilac flowers. Plants can be raised from cuttings taken during May, inserted in a mixture of 50/50 peat and sharp sand, and once rooted grown on in 3-ins pots of potting compost to be planted in the open the following April. Some people like to cut their bushes back to near the woody base every spring to encourage new growth and a tidy habit. The flavour is stronger than that of the annual savory and so use with discretion.

Sorrel

Sorrel was included among leaf salads and is a French herb rich in vitamin C, with leaves shaped like broad arrowheads. I like to chop them to add an acid flavour to the salad bowl. The diarist John Evelyn said the leaves: 'Sharpen the appetite and give so great a sharpness to a salad that the herb should never be omitted.'

Sweet Cicely

Sweet cicely is an erect perennial that will grow 4 or 5 ft high with large divided ferny leaves and heads of white May flowers a bit like those of the cow parsley and these are followed by dark-brown ridged seeds that smell faintly of cloves. It is best to cut off most seed heads before they ripen to prevent over generous self-seeding in the garden. Handsome enough to go in a flower border, sweet cicely is an easy plant that likes a bit of shade and moist soil. Young roots used to be boiled to serve cold in salads, but I would rather chop a few young leaves to add an aniseed flavour to my salad bowl.

(French) Tarragon

Do grow the better quality French *tarragon* rather than the coarser Russian kind. You'll need this perennial as an ingredient of fines herbes, but do also use the chopped leaves on their own in small amounts in salads. Moderately hardy, tarragon needs a sunny position and good drainage, with plenty of well-rotted organic matter added for moisture retention through summer. Clumps are best lifted, divided and replanted in fresh soil every three or four years. Propagation is by removal of a shoot about 10 ins long with a bit of root attached for use as a cutting – the herb does not produce seed. In colder districts it is wise to lift a clump to grow on under cover through winter as an insurance against loss. Tarragon grows 2-3 ft high with branching stems of lance-shaped, dark grey-green leaves. Described as the king of all culinary herbs, this has a distinctive flavour unlike any other plant and in cooking is used especially with poultry. Use the finely chopped leaves to sprinkle over a salad that is going to accompany cold chicken or other poultry, to top a dish of baked and sliced beetroot, and, of course, in fines herbes.

Thyme

Thyme is another of the indispensable culinary herbs, but is used more in cooking than raw; but, do try a little chopped thyme to add zing to your salads – the large leaved form of the common type is by far the best for the kitchen. An attractive little bush for sunny spots on well-drained soil, this is an evergreen for use all year round and should be grown quite close to the kitchen door, perhaps in a trough on the patio or where a slab has been left out of a paved area. As with other aromatic plants, scent and taste will be stronger when grown on dry soil and so leaves from plants grown here should be used with more discretion than those from plants on more fertile land.

Instead of adding the leaves to salads you can add a lovely flavour by steeping a sprig of thyme in salad oil for a period and then removing the herb before the oil is used as a dressing.

(Lemon) Thyme

Like the common thyme a plant of the sunny Mediterranean lands, the *lemon thyme* is another imporant culinary herb. This makes a looser more open bush, with deep pink flowers that come a bit later in summer and are also great favourites with honey bees. Some find the milder lemon flavour of this preferable to that of the common thyme, and you may prefer its finely chopped leaves in salads.

CHAPTER 19

Fresh Fruit

If you want to make your salads really interesting do experiment by adding different kinds of fresh fruit. I started by mixing slices of raw apple into crunchy winter salads and then thought that if they blended so well other fruit might be equally enjoyable. I suppose that any fruit could be mixed with the raw vegetables that comprise our main salad stuffs, but I think those with a slightly tart flavour are a better choice than the very sweet kinds.

Apples

A really ripe 'Bramley Seedling' cooking *apple* that has been in store long enough to mellow is, I believe, far nicer diced or sliced in a salad than is a 'Cox's Orange Pippin', whose sweet taste is admirable with other sweet items in a fresh fruit salad to serve at the end of a meal.

Experiment with apples of different varieties. Dessert varieties with colourful skins like that excellent late season 'Idared' are most attractive if peel is left on, but I always peel a 'Bramley Seedling' thinly. Dual-purpose apples suitable for cooking or dessert like 'Charles Ross' are particularly good in salads but, because they tend to be larger than dessert varieties, you may find that half is ample if there are only two or three to sit down to the meal. The yellow-skinned 'Golden Delicious' and tart green-skinned 'Granny Smith' are two good dessert varieties to use in this way.

Because apple tends to turn brown after being cut up, it's wise to dip your prepared slices or diced pieces into lemon juice to prevent this happening. That adds another fruity flavour and extra vitamin C.

Citrus Fruit

Segments of small *oranges*, *satsumas* and *clementines* and broken segments of larger oranges and *grapefruit*, with all the pith carefully peeled away, are delicious mixed into salads. They are specially valuable in the winter months when fresh ingredients are not so easily obtained and, again, help to provide vitamin C.

Some people use canned *pineapple* in salads and if thoroughly drained of the syrup this can be good, but small pieces of a fresh pineapple are even better.

Grapes

Black *grapes*, preferably halved and stoned, are excellent among the topping on a salad and if you use them at the time of year when shop prices are modest they need not be an extravagant ingredient. I don't think you'll find them too sweet to blend with other salad stuffs, but if in doubt avoid using grapes with beetroot, bite-sized tomatoes or 'Little Gem' lettuce. Instead use them with chicory, shredded cabbage, loose leaf lettuce or watercress and garnish the bowl with a mere suggestion of finely chopped bitter herbs.

Berries

Among our summer soft fruit from the garden my top choice for salads are the little *alpine strawberries*, so easy to raise from seed and to grow as edging plants around a border. Unlike their larger cousins, these don't give big pickings, but you can gather a handful of small fruits over many weeks and with a slightly tart flavour they are splendid for topping the

Figure 47: Alpine strawberry plant with some ripe fruit, some blooms

salad bowl. Try adding the odd tablespoonful of freshly picked *blackcurrants*, a few *redcurrants* stripped off the long strings with a table fork, *blackberries* gathered when only just ripe, or slices of green *gooseberries*, in the same way.

Stone Fruits

Most of those delicious dark *Morello cherries* will find there way into pies or preserves, but do try adding a few stoned and halved fruits to your summer salads. Halved and stoned *damsons* can be used in the same manner a few weeks later in the season.

Bananas

For me, really ripe *bananas* are a bit too sweet for the salad bowl, but a slightly under-ripe fruit sliced over a salad can be delicious and transform a mundane dish into something unusual and exciting.

Melons

Among other fresh fruit from overseas, do make use of those big golden honeydew *melons* that are most often served as a starter or as a dessert. Try chopping melon to blend with a mixture of more conventional salad stuffs, or remove the seeds from a half melon and fill the hollow with a mixture of chopped celery, shredded cos lettuce, diced green pepper and tiny cubes of Edam cheese with a sprinkling of finely chopped herbs. Use this as a starter or as a main course with wholemeal rolls and butter.

Avocados

Avocado pear is super in salad if skin and stone are removed and the sliced flesh is dipped in lemon juice to prevent browning. Try mixing this with broken grapefruit segments on a bed of lettuce leaves topped by tiny tomato wedges and a sprinkling of chopped herbs.

These are a few of my suggestions and if you like to be

143

adventurous, I'm sure you'll be able to think up lots more ways of incorporating fresh fruit into your salads.

CHAPTER 20

Dried Fruit, Preserved Fruit and Nuts

There is a lot of goodness and a lot of flavour in dried fruit and I find that small amounts are superb for blending among my other salad toppings. I said that I preferred slightly tart fresh fruit to mix with raw vegetables and I'll admit that dried fruits are sweet and sugary, but they all seem to blend well with salad stuffs and especially with the more bitter items like chicory and Chinese cabbage, loose leaf lettuce and spinach. Nuts are nutritious and tasty too, and chopped, halved or milled are essential ingredients for anyone aiming at exciting salads.

Fruits

Most dried fruits should be chopped before use and that's specially so with larger ones like dates and prunes. Chopped and pitted *dates* are super mixed into any salad with shredded 'Sugar Loaf'-type chicory as the base, and go well too with shredded 'January King' cabbage and Chinese mung bean shoots. I like to mix cheese and dates in a vegetarian meal. If *prunes* are very shrivelled by drying you may find it best to soak them for an hour or so before chopping and removing the stones, but those sold ready packed in plastic bags that need no soaking can be chopped straightaway to blend in with other salad ingredients. Use them also with shredded cabbage, chopped celery or with grated raw vegetables on a bed of lettuce leaves.

Seedless *raisins* and *sultanas* are both excellent with almost any blend of salad stuffs, whether they are served whole or cut in halves. For a delicious and health-giving winter variation soak these dried fruits for a few hours in enough lemon juice diluted to half strength with hot water to cover. This will make them plump and juicy and

145

so good in a salad – use any leftover juice with olive oil as a dressing.

Both green and black *olives* are splendid for garnishing the salad bowl, or you can chop a tablespoon or so of them and stir into a carton of cottage cheese to top a mixed salad. Sliced pickled *gherkins*, drained from their brine while you are preparing the meal, are also good for mixing into the topping and can be combined with the chopped olives. Canned *pimento* cut into strips makes a colourful garnish and can be arranged in trellis fashion over the salad bowl or platter.

Nuts

Nuts provide lots of goodness and blend admirably with almost any mixture of salad stuffs. Some people use salted or roasted nuts, but I prefer mine to be untreated. You can serve the different kinds alone or mixed together, either chopping the nuts to blend among other salad ingredients or milling them to sprinkle liberally over the bowl as a topping.

If you live in or near the country or have a garden large enough for a *hazel* bush you can have fresh nuts straight from the tree in autumn. Even better are the hazel's close relative, the much larger Kentish cob nuts. Grown in orchards in parts of Kent, this makes a bush or tree like a hazel with the same yellow male catkins that sway in winter breezes and the same tiny crimson female flowers that are followed by those tasty nuts. They are lovely chopped or milled in a salad.

Walnuts make big trees and few of our gardens are large enough to grow at home, but they are not expensive to buy in the shells or ready shelled. Most of these go into cakes or are used to decorate cakes and confectionery, but I believe halved or chopped walnuts make one of the nicest salad toppings of all.

Almonds can be served blanched or unblanched, depending on personal preference. Use them whole as a garnish, chopped to mix into the salad or to blend with cottage cheese with chopped pepper or olives as a topping, or milled as a topping to finish with some finely chopped chives or parsley.

Peanuts can be blanched, but I don't consider that necessary. They are the least expensive nuts to buy and

146

are very good to eat raw, surprisingly proving cheaper to buy shelled than in the shells. Use them whole mixed with seedless raisins to stir into a blend of grated carrot, shredded cabbage, chopped celery and onion rings as a delicious winter meal. Or, mill the peanuts to sprinkle liberally over the salad bowl at any time of year.

Cashew nuts are so good whole or halved that I'm loathe to mill them, but prefer to scatter a handful over a salad just before it goes on the table. *Brazil* nuts are too big to serve in that way and so I prefer to mill them to make a topping. It's almost impossible to shell these nuts without breaking into pieces and so I find it a good idea to use up the broken bits as a milled salad topping.

CHAPTER 21

Flowers

Flower petals could never be considered as main ingredients for a salad, but some of them are perfect for arranging on top of the bowl as a most decorative garnish that adds colour and extra flavour.

I've already suggested *nasturtium* leaves as an addition to summer and autumn salads. Now, I want to suggest using some of the gay yellow, flame and scarlet petals to top your green salads. Use whole blossoms after first making sure there are no earwigs trapped in the long back spurs, or gently break off the petals to scatter over the bowl. After the flowers come big seeds that are sometimes pickled for use as substitute capers. They have a spicy flavour and are very good chopped and served with discretion straight from the plants. I think them especially good to liven up a mixture of the more blandly flavoured items like shredded 'Minicole' cabbage, or sliced white 'Icicle' radishes and tomato on a bed of lettuce.

The *calendula* was given the name of pot marigold because its leaves and flowers were so much used by herbalists and housewives in the old days. The bright orange and yellow petals of this easy hardy annual are ideal for sprinkling over the salad bowl to add a touch of colour and a piquant flavour. Combine them with chopped parsley and you've a showy and tasty garnish.

Strew other herb flowers over your salads, always choosing those of a colour that will contrast with other ingredients. Bright-blue *borage* flowers look well with green and red; the mauvy-blue of *rosemary* flowers with yellow and green; and the deeper-blue of *hyssop* flowers with the orange and gold of calendulas on a green salad.

In spring, try garnishing with a few delicate yellow *primroses* or some purple *violets* for extra special salads. For more mundane occasions, like Monday lunch, garnish liberally with bright-yellow *dandelion* petals – if you gather them from

148

Figure 48: Climbing single nasturtium plant, showing leaves and flower bud

the wild do make sure no herbicide has been used in the area of late!

Marrows and courgettes have such showy golden blooms that I always feel it's a shame to waste all the abundance of male blooms, easily recognised because they have no embryo fruit behind their petals. If your plants have more male blooms than are needed to pollinate the females, gather them to use as a bold decoration for your salad bowl. The similar but very much smaller *cucumber* flowers are good too, especially when mixed with diced green pepper as a topping for a mixed salad.

Lastly, I must suggest *red rose* petals, something readily available in almost every English garden in summer. They are super for adding a dash of colour to green salads in those midsummer weeks before home-grown tomatoes have begun to ripen.

CHAPTER 22

Salad Dressings

Simple dressings are the kind I like best for salads, for I want to enjoy the flavours of the raw vegetables and fruit and not to eat them smothered in mayonnaise or some other concoction. When I see bowls of ready-made salads on sale in delicatessen shops I'm appalled by the high percentage of dressing in them all.

Of course you can save time and trouble by using bottled salad cream or mayonnaise from the shops and that is a handy aid for picnics if used with discretion – but, too much can spoil a meal. And as for calories, that's one thing to watch with all salad dressings, for while a mixed meal of raw vegetables, fruit and nuts can be ideal for anyone trying to lose weight the good it does can be counteracted by a rich mayonnaise. So, if you are slimming watch the ingredients of the dressing as closely as your waistline.

Very often the only dressing I'll add to my salad is a little olive oil, usually a dessertspoonful per person, though the amount depends a lot on the ingredients of the salad. Beetroot and grated carrot absorb a lot of oil, where a green leafy salad or one made mainly from shredded cabbage and chopped celery needs very little.

French Salad Dressing

The classical *French salad dressing* of one part wine vinegar to three parts olive oil plus salt and pepper to taste is splendid for any tossed salad and can be varied by adding a number of ingredients. Make the basic dressing by placing the oil and vinegar, salt and freshly ground black pepper in a screw top jar and shaking well. This will keep for ages in the fridge and so you can make up enough for a week or fortnight at a time. For variations add a little crushed garlic, a little powdered or made mustard, a small amount of Worcester sauce, a teaspoonful of tomato puree, finely grated horseradish or some chopped anchovies. Some cooks add dried or chopped fresh herbs, but I prefer to add these direct to the salad before adding the dressing.

In French dressing you can replace the vinegar with lemon juice and this gives a lovely sharp fruity flavour that I like. Alternatively, you can use orange juice – and this is good with green salads that contain some fruit.

Yoghurt Dressing

Sometimes I add *natural yoghurt* to my salads and you can use this also as a dressing, adding a little paprika before serving. With green salads, try a dressing made from a carton (5 ozs) of natural yoghurt mixed with half a tablespoonful of wine vinegar and salt and pepper to taste.

Another basic yoghurt dressing can be made by mixing a carton of natural yoghurt with two tablespoonsful of the top of the milk, three teaspoonsful of lemon juice, one level teaspoon of caster sugar, salt and pepper. First beat the cream, then the fruit juice and finally the sugar into the yoghurt, season and cool for 15 minutes before serving. You can add different things to this, and chopped herbs often do go in, but I prefer the simple dressing on its own.

Soured Cream Dressing

Soured cream makes a good salad dressing if you beat a carton (5 ozs) well together with a tablespoonful of milk and a tablespoonful of lemon juice or wine vinegar, stir in a good half teaspoonful of icing sugar and season to taste with salt and pepper. Add more milk if a thinner dressing is needed and cool for 15 minutes before serving.

I've seen lots of things used to vary this, including all kinds of fruit and vegetables or herbs – that I would add to the salad bowl itself. Additions I do like include one teaspoonful of made mustard for a salad to serve with beef or ham; one teaspoonful of finely grated lemon rind for salads to serve with poultry or fish; two level teaspoonsful of finely grated horseradish for salads to serve with cold beef; or a tablespoon-ful of tomato purée for a salad to serve with eggs, cheese or poultry.

Salad Dressings

Tomato Dressing

In summer when *tomatoes* are plentiful, perhaps in your own garden, you can make a good salad dressing by sieving several very ripe fruits to given seven or eight tablespoonsful of juicy pulp. Season this with salt and pepper, add a tablespoonful of Worcester sauce and two tablespoonsful of lemon juice.

Mayonnaise

Home-made *mayonnaise* will keep in a screw top jar in the fridge for several days and so there's no need to make it just before the meal. Mixing slowly when you are not rushed is the secret of success. Break an egg yolk into a bowl, add a half teaspoonful each of salt, pepper and dry mustard, beat until smooth and then with a wooden spoon add olive oil from a quarter pint a drop at a time and whisk vigorously until you have a thick emulsion. Add the remaining oil a little more quickly while still whisking and finally thin with a tablespoonful of wine vinegar or lemon juice.

The basic recipe can be varied by adding chopped herbs to give a green mayonnaise; tomato purée or beetroot juice for pink mayonnaise; or finely chopped capers and gherkins for tartare sauce to serve with salads to accompany grilled fish. You can replace the vinegar or lemon juice with water for a less pungent sauce, or add whipped cream for a richer mayonnaise.

You'll find plenty of choice of salad dressings in recipe books, but if you have created interesting salads I don't think you will need anything more elaborate than these basic dressings that will allow the flavours of the salad ingredients to be enjoyed to the full.

Salads for Every Month of the Year

JANUARY

Shredded 'Winter White' cabbage for a base topped by a pile of finely grated carrot, diced dessert apple (dipped in lemon juice to prevent discolouring), sliced leek and thinly sliced celeriac. Garnish with chopped dates and walnuts.

Chinese cabbage shredded for a base, then shredded Brussels sprouts, sliced tomatoes and rings from a medium-sized onion attractively arranged. Garnish with finely chopped parsley.

Diced white 'Mino Early' mild winter radish, swede, russet apple, chopped onion and chicory all mixed together in a bowl with a carton of natural yoghurt. Garnish with halved black grapes and blanched almonds.

Mung bean shoots, shredded heart of 'January King' cabbage, chopped onion and celery all mixed together in a big bowl or on individual plates. Garnish with chopped red pepper to add colour.

A simple salad made from celery hearts, salad rape, quartered tomatoes and sliced baked beetroot arranged in separate piles on a big platter. Leave room in the centre for a small bowl of mayonnaise, or a pile of natural cottage cheese.

'Sugar Loaf' chicory shredded for the base topped by generous amounts of salad rape and alfalfa. Garnish with corn salad, winter purslane and land cress leaves plus segments from a satsuma.

Chopped celery and English 'Golden Delicious' apple mixed with mung bean shoots, sliced pickled onions and blanched almonds. Garnish with seedless raisins.

Hothouse lettuce torn up in a bowl and mixed with sprigs of watercress, spicy fenugreek shoots and salad rape. Garnish with half a red pepper chopped into small pieces and a tablespoonful or two of milled peanuts.

'Winter White' cabbage finely shredded and mixed with a chopped onion (the colder the day the larger the onion), diced 'Bramley Seedling' cooking apple and a carton of natural yoghurt. For colour garnish with small cubes of Red Leicester cheese and chopped dates, plus a sprinkling of any evergreen herb leaves you can find.

Mixed sprouted seeds – mung and adzuki beans, alfalfa and fenugreek. Mix with two diced apples of a red-skinned dessert variety, in a bowl that has first been rubbed around with a crushed clove of garlic. Garnish with chopped prunes.

A green salad made from a mixture of small sideshoots of 'Pentland Brig' kale, alfalfa, chopped Welsh onions, torn up very young spinach beet leaves and small sprigs of parsley on a bed of finely shredded red cabbage. Garnish with halved and seeded green grapes.

Half a head of celery chopped and mixed with chopped chicory ('Sugar Loaf', or a forced chicon from the shops) and half segments of grapefruit (from which all the pith has been removed). Garnish with a generous helping of sultanas (scalded to make them swell up) and a small handful of peanuts.

FEBRUARY

Two different dishes today. One filled with diced baked beetroot mixed with a carton of natural yoghurt and then garnished with chopped chives; the other filled with a mixture of alfalfa, diced russet apple and finely chopped shallot and then garnished with chopped parsley.

A mixed green salad made from shredded Brussels sprouts, a punnet of salad rape, a diced half green pepper, a diced 'Granny Smith' apple, some chopped Welsh onions and half a dozen stoned and halved green grapes.

Individual servings with, on each plate, several endive leaves, four or five segments of satsuma, a helping of mung bean shoots, a celery heart and a few whole stoned raisins.

Generous helpings of finely grated carrot served on individual plates among a mixture of one small shallot and two Brussels sprouts finely chopped for each person. Top with corn salad and land cress leaves plus just a few thyme leaves for a subtle herb flavour. For a variation try adding a tablespoonful of baked beans to each serving.

'Winter White' cabbage, a fair-sized onion, a large 'Crispin' apple and a few Brazil nuts all chopped quite small and mixed with a carton of soured cream and some adzuki bean shoots. For colour, garnish with a tomato chopped into small pieces.

Entertaining tonight and so a salad made from all bought ingredients. A hothouse lettuce torn up and mixed with a thinly sliced half cucumber, and slices from a large Jaffa orange from which all the pith has been removed. Add some black olives and serve in a glass bowl for best effect.

A bunch of watercress broken into small pieces and tossed together with some finely shredded Brussels sprouts and a finely shredded shallot. Serve on a platter topped by a generous amount of finely grated carrot and garnish with chop suey green leaves.

Shredded red cabbage, chopped pink celery, mung bean shoots and thin rings cut from a medium-sized onion mixed together with a level teaspoonful of caraway seeds. Garnish with small wedges cut from a red-skinned dessert apple.

A very crunchy salad today with a mixture of tiny sprigs of cauliflower, a carrot cut into thin inch-long strips, sliced leeks, diced celeriac and a handful of peanuts. Garnish with chopped lemon balm leaves.

A mixed green salad made from whatever is available – perhaps young spinach leaves torn up and mixed with small sprigs of 'Pentland Brig' kale, watercress, corn salad, salad rocket, winter purslane, chop suey greens and young parsley leaves in a bowl that has been rubbed with garlic. For garnish – sliced button mushrooms and small wedges of tomato.

A long beetroot baked, then diced and mixed with a carton of

155

soured cream. Pile this in the centre of a big platter and garnish with a tablespoonful of seedless raisins. Surround the pile with leaves from a head of endive mixed with salad rape and topped by chopped shallot leaves.

Red cabbage shredded very finely and mixed with thinly sliced shallot and coarsely grated dessert apple. Top with milled mixed nuts and chervil leaves.

MARCH

Grated ingredients today all blended together in a bowl with half a green pepper that has been deseeded and chopped into tiny pieces. A good basic mix can consist of four parts of finely grated carrot to one part each of finely grated parsnip, swede, 'China Rose' winter radish, onion and 'Granny Smith' apple. Garnish with a few chopped leaves of mixed herbs.

A bed of lettuce leaves arranged on a big platter or on individual plates. On top a mixture of chopped celery and diced cucumber garnished with halved black grapes.

A chicon of chicory shredded and mixed with chopped seakale and broken segments of grapefruit in a bowl garnished with chopped dates and sliced banana.

A green salad made by mixing all the best pieces from a bunch of watercress with purple sprouting broccoli tips, plenty of corn salad leaves, small sprigs of parsley and several spring onion-like shallots. Break the ingredients up and toss together then garnish with bright-yellow petals from a handful of dandelion flowers.

Rub the inside of a salad bowl with garlic. Fill with a mixture of mung bean shoots, diced 'Golden Delicious' apple, chopped seakale, and tiny sprigs of white sprouting broccoli, or small bits broken off from a cauliflower intended for tomorrow's hot vegetable. Garnish the salad with chopped chervil leaves and sultanas that have been soaked in 50/50 lemon juice and hot water.

Young spinach leaves, first of the blanched dandelion leaves, adzuki bean shoots, and a head of endive broken up and mixed together with some orange segments. Garnish with a tablespoonful each of chopped parsley and seedless raisins. You may like to rub the salad bowl with garlic before filling.

A bed of lettuce leaves topped by a mixture of finely grated carrot, coarsely grated 'Bramley Seedling' apple, a carton of natural cottage cheese and small amounts of grated 'Black Spanish' winter radish and celeriac. Garnish with black olives.

A lettuce torn up and mixed with the best of a bunch of watercress that has been broken into small sprigs. (For a salad like this you don't need hearted lettuce, but can use thinnings from a seed bed in the greenhouse.) Add a can of pineapple chunks, that have been well drained, and then garnish with cashew nuts.

A mixture of pale ingredients with a chopped chicon of chicory mixed with blanched dandelion leaves, stems of salsify and scorzonera and mung bean shoots. Stir into this a couple of thinly sliced 'Idared' apples with the bright-red skins left on and garnish with walnut halves.

The first of the mustard and cress from the greenhouse tossed together with torn up lettuce leaves, lots of small sprigs of parsley, tiny spears of purple sprouting broccoli and a sliced leek. Garnish with orange segments.

Rub the inside of a salad bowl with garlic and fill with a mixture of sprouted seeds – adzuki, alphatoco and mung bean shoots, alfalfa and fenugreek. Stir into this a handful of peanuts and a sliced, slightly under-ripe banana.

A small head of 'Florence' fennel chopped and mixed with the best small sprigs of a bunch of watercress and half a deseeded, diced red pepper. Serve in a salad bowl rubbed with garlic and garnish with cashew nuts.

APRIL

Lashings of torn up lettuce grown for use as cut-and-come-again leaf salad, tossed together with mung bean shoots, chopped shallots grown as a substitute for spring onions, dandelion and land cress leaves, plus a couple of sliced radishes for each person. Top the mixture with tiny cubes of Dutch Edam cheese and a tablespoonful of sultanas.

Shredded 'Winter White' cabbage for the base topped by a pile of finely grated carrot surrounded by a deep ring of mustard and cress, with whole round red radishes dotted every couple of inches round on top. Garnish the carrot with a thick sprinkling of mixed chopped chervil and chives.

One of the first warm spring days and so a picnic lunch for a trip to the country. For each person take a salad, in a cottage cheese tub. For the basic mix I suggest a couple of heaped tablespoonsful of finely grated carrot, a finely sliced pickling-sized shallot, a heaped teaspoonful of chopped parsley, half a 'Crispin' apple, diced and dipped in lemon juice to prevent discolouring, and a couple of heaped tablesoonsful of adzuki bean shoots. Fill the tub and pour in a dessertspoonful of olive oil as dressing. If you like, you can then hollow out the salad and place a dessertspoonful of homemade apple chutney in the centre. Serve with crusty bread rolls bought on the way to eat with butter, hunks of Cheddar cheese and sliced ham.

Sticks of imported celery mixed with the first 'Suzan' lettuce, 'White Lisbon' spring onions and 'Cherry Belle' radishes from the greenhouse border. No chopping or tossing, but each item displayed separately on a platter, or on individual plates.

A green salad made from home-grown mustard and cress, thinnings from the lettuce seed bed, blanched dandelion leaves, sprigs of 'Pentland Brig' kale, salad rocket and chop suey green leaves. Top with sliced button mushrooms and halved red radishes.

Small sprigs from a cauliflower, thinly sliced 'Idared' apple with the skin left on, chopped seakale, chopped blanched stems of salsify, chopped leaves of Chinese leeks (chives) and some mung bean shoots tossed together in a bowl. Garnish with chopped lemon balm leaves.

Easter nest salads on individual plates today. For each one a big cabbage lettuce leaf with a pile of alfalfa shoots arranged on it in a ring to look like a bird's nest. Line this with thinly sliced cucumber and fill with four or five round red radishes for the eggs.

Finely grated carrot mixed with chopped seakale, spicy fenugreek shoots, thinly sliced leek and small spears of purple sprouting broccoli. Garnish liberally with chopped parsley and some blanched almonds. Serve sliced beetroot as a separate dish, garnishing this with a finely shredded sorrel leaf.

An economy salad today, but nourishing and delicious. A big pile of ferny true cress leaves grown on past the familiar seed leaf stage, with some torn up young spinach leaves, shallot tops cut into $\frac{1}{2}$-in lengths, small spears of white sprouting broccoli, small sprigs of parsley, and a thinly sliced 'Idared' apple – dipped first in lemon juice to prevent browning and allowing half an apple per person. Toss all the ingredients together and garnish with a good tablespoonful of peanuts.

Toss together a teacupful of frozen or tinned petit pois peas, a small bunch of spring onions chopped into short lengths, a punnet of salad rape and a small bunch of land cress. Serve this blend on a bed of lettuce leaves and garnish with small wedges of tomato and sliced hard-boiled eggs.

A small cauliflower coarsely grated and mixed with a grated 'Bramley Seedling' cooking apple, and finely chopped fair-sized onion, then stirred into a bowl with an 8 ozs tub of natural cottage cheese. Add to the mixture a couple of quartered radishes per person and some chopped dates.

Outer leaves of a 'Winter Density' lettuce torn up for the base topped by a big pile of true leaf cress surrounded by a ring of small sprigs of watercress and halved 'Cherry Belle' radishes. Garnish with primrose flowers that have had the stalks removed so they sit open-faced on top of the cress.

MAY

A bed of cabbage lettuce leaves topped by a mixture of half a sliced cucumber and a bunch of watercress that has been broken into small pieces. Garnish with cold cooked asparagus tips and sunshine-yellow dandelion flower petals.

Rub the inside of a salad bowl with garlic and fill with tossed seed leaf mustard, ferny true leaf cress, fenugreek shoots, a finely chopped onion and a few chopped lovage leaves. Cut a skinned, beefsteak tomato into cubes and mix in with the green salad. Garnish with walnut halves.

A bed of lettuce thinnings torn up and tossed together with

spinach thinnings, a generous helping of seed leaf cress, some sprigs of watercress, chopped 'White Lisbon' onions and a few chopped lemon balm leaves. Garnish with orange calendula flower petals.

A no-nonsense salad that is easy to pack for a picnic. One plump 'Winter Density' lettuce heart, an 'Idared' dessert apple, two or three sticks of imported celery and a large pickled onion for each person.

A cabbage lettuce torn up and mixed with a thinly sliced firm banana, several chopped salad onions, a generous helping of seed leaf cress and a few torn up dandelion leaves. Garnish with peanuts.

Quartered cabbage lettuce minus the outside leaves arranged on individual plates with a pile of seed leaf mustard, four plump radishes and a couple of spring onions for each person. Add a good dollop of natural cottage cheese that has been mixed with fresh chopped chives and parsley.

A small can of baked beans, finely chopped spring cabbage heart, a diced cooking apple and thinly sliced large onion all stirred together. Serve in a bowl topped by small cubes of Dutch Edam cheese and a tablespoonful of chopped chervil.

Small sprigs of cauliflower, the first baby carrot thinnings, an onion cut into thin rings, a bunch of watercress broken into small sprigs and a tablespoonful of seedless raisins all mixed together in a bowl. Garnish with chopped fennel leaves.

Rub the salad bowl with garlic and fill with a 'Winter Density' lettuce torn into bite-sized pieces and four good-sized tomatoes cut into small wedges. Stir in a tablespoonful of fines herbes and then garnish with mauve-blue rosemary flowers.

A cabbage lettuce torn up to make a base topped by a blend of salad rape, diced cucumber and chopped spring onions. Garnish with sliced green gooseberries and orange calendula flower petals.

Salad kebabs for a picnic or supper party. Different skewers can contain different items, but I suggest inch cubes of Cheddar cheese, whole red radishes, florets of cauliflower, pickled onions, ham slices cut into two and rolled tightly, baby raw carrots, inch slices of cucumber cut into halves so the skewer goes in from skin to centre, and stoned dates. Serve with crusty French bread and butter.

Chopped 'Winter Density' lettuce leaves mixed with a tomato cut into small wedges, a chopped bunch of 'White Lisbon' onions, sliced button mushrooms and a heaped tablespoonful of chopped mixed fresh herbs. Garnish with halved black olives.

JUNE

Strawberries don't have to be served with sugar and cream! Try quartered strawberries mixed with torn up cabbage lettuce leaves and diced cucumber, eaten with new potatoes garnished with finely chopped mint leaves and cold chicken or ham.

Small florets of cauliflower, tiny whole new carrots, small round red radishes, very young raw broad beans and chopped salad onions all mixed together in a bowl. Garnish with a tiny sprinkling of chopped thyme leaves and blue flowers of the hardy annual borage.

A cos lettuce torn up and tossed together with a few chopped sorrel leaves, several tablespoonsful each of chopped chives and parsley. Just before serving add sliced cooked young baby beetroot.

Young Swiss chard leaves, true leaf ferny cress, lettuce leaves cut at 2-3 ins high, chopped green tops of salad onions, a few chopped lovage leaves, some torn up nasturtium leaves and several tablespoonsful of raw young green peas tossed together. Garnish the bowl with small orange segments.

A bed of soft butterhead cabbage lettuce leaves topped by a mixture of equal amounts of diced cucumber and diced Dutch Edam cheese. Garnish with wedges of tomato and a sprinkling of chopped chervil.

Torn up lettuce leaves, chopped salad onions and a punnet of salad rape tossed together in a bowl that has first been rubbed with garlic. Stir in a few sliced button mushrooms and garnish liberally with bright-red alpine strawberries.

161

A base of crisphead lettuce torn up into bite-sized pieces. Top this with a mixture of diced cold cooked chicken and melon cut into ½-in cubes. Garnish with small wedges of tomato and a sprinkling of finely chopped summer savory.

Two soft cabbage lettuce leaves on each person's plate, laid one in the other to form a saucer. Cut the top off a good-sized tomato for each person, scoop out the centre and replace with a mixture of the tomato pulp, grated cheese and finely chopped parsley. Stand the stuffed tomato on the lettuce saucer and garnish with a thick slice of cucumber placed on edge to look like a handle for the tomato basket.

A bed of pale crisphead lettuce leaves on a large platter with, piled in the centre, a mixture of diced cooked beetroot and new potatoes stirred together with a carton of yoghurt, topped with a few sprigs of parsley. Serve whole radishes as a garnish on top of the lettuce.

Baby raw carrots, small radishes, young raw broad beans and peas all mixed together and served on a bed of lettuce in a bowl that has first been rubbed with garlic. Garnish with chopped fennel.

A crisphead 'Webbs Wonderful'-type lettuce torn up and mixed with a lot of watercress sprigs. Add one-third of a cucumber diced small and garnish with blue borage flowers, and a few tiny sprigs of mint.

Shredded 'Hispi' cabbage heart mixed with very thinly sliced young 'Snowball' white turnips and carrot thinnings and a heaped tablespoonful of chopped parsley. Garnish with a couple of tablespoonsful of young green peas and a generous helping of chopped chives – finish off with a few freshly gathered nasturtium petals.

JULY

A small cucumber – or a large half – diced and mixed with a level tablespoonful of chopped mint and a carton of natural yoghurt. Serve on a bed of crisphead lettuce leaves.

A cos lettuce torn up and mixed with a punnet of salad rape, two or three chopped 'White Lisbon' onions and two courgettes that have been cut into thin slices – the gold-skinned varieties look better in salad than the more usual green. Garnish with chopped chervil and a heaped tablespoonful of sultanas (that have been soaked overnight in enough 50/50 lemon juice and water to cover).

Allowing one good-sized fruit for each person, slice tomatoes and arrange on a big plate. Sprinkle on top a tablespoonful of very finely chopped shallot and a teaspoonful of chopped sweet basil leaves. Serve lettuce hearts on a separate dish.

'Red Salad Bowl' frilly lettuce leaves arranged on a platter for the base. On this a pile of diced beetroot mixed with a carton of natural yoghurt (mix half an hour before serving so the yoghurt turns pink). Garnish with small strawberries, cut into halves.

Young Swiss chard leaves, lettuce thinnings and several salad onions chopped together with some shredded cabbage heart and a heaped tablespoonful of chopped parsley. Garnish with a handful of fresh ripe blackcurrants.

Salads on individual plates, with on each one two soft cabbage lettuce leaves laid in one another to form a saucer. In this pile a mixture of diced cucumber and melon garnished with tiny sprigs of mint and surrounded by a ring of small wedges of tomato.

A lettuce torn up and mixed with a large onion cut into thin rings and a heaped tablespoonful each of chopped chervil, common fennel and parsley. Garnish the bowl with a few flame flowers of the single climbing nasturtium.

A crisphead lettuce torn up and mixed just before serving with several diced beetroot and a handful of stoned Morello cherries. (Black dessert cherries can be used instead, but I believe the tart cooking variety are nicer in a salad.)

Some carrots are large enough to grate now, so grate a plump root finely and blend with a grated white turnip of golf ball size, a coarsely grated medium-sized onion, some whole peanuts and a carton of natural cottage cheese plus a heaped tablespoonful of seedless raisins. Serve individual portions of the mixture on beds of frilly 'Salad Bowl' lettuce leaves.

A big beefsteak tomato of a variety like 'Super Marmande' cut into $\frac{1}{2}$-in slices. Lay one slice for each person on a saucer made from two soft butterhead cabbage lettuce leaves and in the centre of the tomato place a pile of natural cottage cheese topped by a whole round red radish. Garnish liberally with a mixture of chopped fines herbes.

A crisphead 'Webbs Wonderful' lettuce torn up and mixed with a sliced half cucumber, some walnut halves and a few chopped lemon balm leaves. Garnish with whole loganberries just before serving.

Salad served in four separate dishes, each topped by chopped herbs. Sliced tomatoes topped by chopped basil; sliced cucumber sprinkled with chopped parsley; sliced beetroot topped by a little chopped lemon thyme; 'Little Gem' lettuce hearts sprinkled with chopped common fennel.

AUGUST

Finely chopped ballhead cabbage mixed with cold cooked sliced runner beans and a handful of whole bite-sized 'Sweet 100' tomatoes in a bowl that has first been rubbed with garlic. For extra flavour and goodness, stir in two heaped table-spoonsful of finely chopped parsley just before serving.

A salad flan, with a cheese pastry case baked blind and allowed to cool well before filling. In the centre place a tomato almost cut into wedges so that the pieces open out like a flower. In rings out from this arrange green peas (raw or cooked), sliced cucumber and wedges of tomato. Garnish with sprigs of watercress. Serve lettuce hearts in a separate dish.

Diced baked beetroot, diced cucumber and a very finely chopped shallot stirred together with a carton of natural yoghurt and left for half an hour to turn slightly pink. Serve the mixture on a bed of loose leaf lettuce and garnish with whole fresh raspberries and a tiny sprinkling of chopped French tarragon leaves.

A cos lettuce torn up and tossed together with several chopped salad onions, a handful of ripe blackcurrants, a diced ridge cucumber and a few chopped lemon balm leaves. Garnish the mixed salad with a few blue hyssop flowers.

164

Finely shredded cabbage heart from a 'Minicole' head mixed with a coarsely grated onion, a bunch of watercress broken into small sprigs and two heaped tablespoonsful of chopped parsley. Serve sliced tomatoes topped by a sprinkling of chopped anise leaves as a separate dish.

An avocado pear peeled, diced and dipped in lemon juice, then mixed with a carton of soured cream and equal amounts of diced melon and cucumber. Pile the mixture into individual portions on soft butterhead cabbage lettuce leaves and garnish with small wedges of tomato.

Cold cooked sweet corn kernels, whole baby carrots and sliced stringless dwarf beans tossed together and served on a bed of loose leaf 'Grand Rapids' lettuce. Garnish liberally with chopped chives.

A generous dish of sliced tomatoes topped by a very finely chopped onion and a sprinkling of chopped mint leaves. In a second dish a torn up 'Webbs Wonderful' crisphead lettuce mixed with a small white turnip cut into thin slices and a tablespoonful of chopped common fennel leaves.

Shredded 'Minicole' cabbage mixed with a chopped onion and diced pepper – either a whole pepper of one colour, or some green, some red, some yellow. Serve in a bowl that has been rubbed with garlic and garnish generously with chopped parsley and a mere sprinkling of chopped dill leaves.

Golden tomatoes make a change from the usual red varieties. Try cutting several 'Golden Sunrise' tomatoes into wedges and mixing with a sliced 'Golden Zucchini' courgette and a diced 'Goldstar' yellow pepper. Serve on a bed of loose leaf 'Salad Bowl' lettuce and garnish with tiny sprigs of parsley.

A crisphead lettuce torn up and mixed with a chopped small head of 'Florence' fennel and whole 'Sweet 100' tomatoes. Serve in a bowl rubbed with garlic and garnish with whole black olives.

Diced baked beetroot, diced 'Discovery' dessert apple and a diced ridge cucumber tossed together and left for half an hour until the apple and cucumber turn faintly pink. Serve the mixture on a bed of torn up crisphead lettuce and garnish with walnut halves.

165

SEPTEMBER

For each person a small apple-shaped cucumber with the top cut off. Scoop out the pulp and mix with a finely chopped shallot, a diced red pepper, a dessertspoonful of chopped dill leaves and a few tablespoonsful of soured cream. Fill the cucumber cases and serve on a bed of watercress garnished with sprigs of mint.

A simple salad made from torn up leaves of the 'Deep Red' loose leaf lettuce mixed with diced baked beetroot, a carton of natural yoghurt and a handful of fresh raw ripe blackberries. Garnish with more blackberries.

Rub a salad bowl with garlic, and toss together torn up loose leaf lettuce, ferny true leaf cress, several chopped 'White Lisbon' onions, half a green pepper that has been deseeded and diced, a sliced ridge cucumber and a generous helping of small sprigs of calabrese green sprouting broccoli. Garnish with 'Sweet 100' tomatoes.

A head of blanched curly endive torn up and mixed with one or two cubed 'Marmande' or 'Super Marmande' beefsteak tomatoes plus a ridge cucumber cut into $\frac{1}{8}$-in slices. Just before serving, mix in a handful of shiny, ripe purple damsons.

A generous pile of home-grown mustard and cress for the base. On top of this one sliced tomato for each person garnished with a very finely sliced shallot and a big spoonful of fines herbes. Add quartered hard-boiled eggs as an optional extra.

Dip several large tomatoes in boiling water so skins come away easily and then chop quite small. Mix with several tablespoonsful of raw green peas, a medium-sized onion cut into thin rings and an apple-shaped cucumber cut into small pieces. Serve the mixture on a bed of cabbage lettuce leaves and garnish with tiny sprigs of mint.

Emerald and gold today with a bed of torn up outer lettuce leaves topped by a mixture of cold cooked sweet corn kernels, chopped cooked yellow waxpod 'Wachs Goldperle' dwarf beans, sliced 'Yellow Perfection' golden tomatoes, 'Gold Rush' courgette thinly sliced, and $\frac{1}{2}$-in cubes of Dutch Edam cheese. Garnish liberally with chopped parsley.

166

Diced baked beetroot mixed with a carton of natural cottage cheese and left for half an hour to turn pink. Pile this in the centre of a platter surrounded by frilly loose leaf lettuce leaves and either wedges cut from an apple-shaped or a sliced ridge cucumber. Garnish with ferny chervil leaves.

Cold boiled potatoes diced and mixed with cold cooked sliced runner beans, diced cooked carrots, diced raw cucumber and a carton of soured cream. Garnish the blend generously with chopped chives. Serve whole cooked 'Little Ball' beetroots garnished sparingly with chopped summer savory leaves in a separate dish.

The Oriental look with a salad made from shredded Chinese cabbage, mung bean shoots, thin slices from one of the big Japanese 'Mino Early' winter radishes, topped by chopped leaves of the garlic-flavoured Chinese leeks (sometimes called Chinese chives), the chrysanthemum-like leaves of chop suey greens and a can of well-drained mandarin orange segments.

A cos lettuce torn up and mixed with the best of a chopped head of self-blanching celery, a handful of fresh hazelnuts and a handful of green, seedless sultana grapes.

A head of 'Florence' fennel chopped and mixed with sprigs from a bunch of watercress, a red pepper that has been deseeded and cut into thin rings, and some whole black olives. Garnish with blanched almonds. If you like, rub the bowl with a crushed clove of garlic.

OCTOBER

Four separate dishes: diced baked beetroot topped by a sprinkling of chopped leaves of the common fennel; sliced cucumber topped by blue borage flowers; wedges of tomato topped by chopped sweet marjoram leaves; a punnet of salad rape sprinkled with bright orange calendula petals.

A head of self-blanching celery chopped, mixed with a handful of fresh hazelnuts and two or three chopped and peeled 'Conference' pears. Garnish with fresh autumn raspberries.

A cos lettuce torn up and mixed with half a yellow pepper that has been deseeded and chopped into small pieces, a good handful of small tomatoes cut into quarters and several chopped 'Paris Silverskin' pickling onions. Garnish with small sprigs of parsley.

A salad base made from shredded Chinese 'Sampan' cabbage tossed together with a bunch of watercress broken into sprigs. For topping, a generous pile of sliced tomatoes garnished with walnut halves and a heaped tablespoonful of fines herbes.

'Deep Red' loose leaf lettuce leaves used to line a platter topped by a broken up head of curly blanched endive and a sliced avocado pear (dipped in lemon juice to preserve the colour). Garnish with red grapes, or fresh autumn raspberries.

The best part of a head of 'American Green' celery (use outer stalks for making soup), one large or two medium-sized 'Charles Ross' dual-purpose apples, and a ridge cucumber – all chopped and mixed together with a handful of peanuts. Garnish with some plump, scalded sultanas.

Half of one of the first heads of 'Sugar Loaf' chicory shredded for the base. Top this with late runner beans, sliced cooked and cold; two or three chopped small 'Conference' pears; and a few quartered small end-of-season tomatoes. Garnish with a tablespoonful of chopped leaves of the common fennel.

Part of a head of Chinese cabbage shredded for the base topped by a mixture of a chopped head of 'Florence' fennel and quartered small tomatoes. Serve in a bowl rubbed with garlic and garnish with a few finely chopped sweet basil leaves. Allow at least two tomatoes for each person.

A bed of loose leaf lettuce leaves topped by chopped sticks of green celery mixed with a handful of stoned green grapes and a half pepper that has been deseeded and diced – for this salad, green looks more attractive than red. Garnish with golden-yellow calendula petals.

A large tomato for each person. Cut a slice off the top, scoop out the pulp and refill with the pulp mixed with canned tuna fish and finely chopped cucumber, topped with a sprinkling of chopped dill leaves. Serve the filled tomatoes on a bed of watercress. If you have some late summer radishes, cut them in halves and use to garnish the watercress.

Shredded Brussels sprouts, a bunch of corn salad leaves, diced cucumber, cooked cold sliced runner beans from the late row, quartered summer radishes and a heaped tablespoonful of chopped chervil all tossed together in a bowl rubbed with garlic. Garnish with quartered small tomatoes or with small wedges from a large tomato.

Serve this arranged on individual plates. Allow for each person a 'Density' lettuce heart, several central sticks from a head of self-blanching celery, a tomato cut into wedges or quarters and a portion of natural cottage cheese that has been mixed with fines herbes, allowing two heaped tablespoonsful of the leaves to a $\frac{1}{2}$ lb tub of cheese.

NOVEMBER

Plenty of tomatoes ripened in a cupboard indoors from the last of the outdoor crop, but none firm enough to serve whole. Instead, dip in boiling water so skins slip away easily, roughly chop and mix with cold chicken and finely chopped parsley, then serve in individual portions on a bed of lettuce leaves. Garnish with triangles made by cutting unpeeled slices of cucumber into four.

Serve a mixture of shredded 'Sugar Loaf' chicory, chopped 'White Lisbon' onions and chopped 'American Green' celery in a salad bowl and garnish with walnut halves. Serve sliced baked beetroot in a separate dish and garnish this with just a few chopped lemon thyme leaves.

Shredded Chinese cabbage mixed with a generous amount of roughly chopped skinned tomatoes, a sliced leek and two or three tablespoonsful of finely chopped parsley. Garnish with two or three chopped green nasturtium seeds.

On each person's plate two cabbage lettuce leaves laid one in the other to form a saucer for a mixture made from two sticks of green celery chopped and blended with four or five chopped cobnuts and half an 'Egremont Russet' apple that has been sliced and dipped in lemon juice to prevent discolouring. Garnish each plate with a chopped dessert date.

Bunches of land cress, chop suey green and corn salad leaves tossed together with torn up lettuce, young spinach and

169

nasturtium leaves, chopped leaves of the Chinese garlic-flavoured leeks (chives), half a red pepper (deseeded and diced) and a number of blanched almonds.

Finely grated carrot piled on a bed of salad rape and sliced leek. Garnish with very thin slices of 'Black Spanish' winter radish and chopped cobnuts.

A very simple salad made by mixing shredded 'Minicole' cabbage with a carton of natural yoghurt, a diced half red pepper, chopped dates and walnuts.

Shredded 'Sugar Loaf' chicory mixed with segments from two or three small oranges and a handful of black grapes that will counteract the slightly bitter taste. Garnish with sprigs of watercress.

Shredded Chinese cabbage mixed with a finely chopped onion for the base. Top this with a generous pile of alfalfa and a smaller central pile of finely grated carrot. Garnish with salad burnet leaves and a tablespoonful of seedless raisins.

On individual plates serve for each person two sticks of celery, two quarters of hard-boiled egg, a small pile of alfalfa shoots, a portion of diced baked beetroot, about one tablespoonful of natural cottage cheese and a large pickled shallot.

A bed of torn up lettuce leaves topped by a pile of finely grated carrot surrounded by a ring of tiny piles of finely grated 'Black Spanish' winter radish, swede, raw beetroot, parsnip and milled peanuts. Garnish the carrot with a blend of chopped chives and parsley leaves.

On individual plates, make cabbage leaf saucers from the pale central leaves of a savoy cabbage. Pile onto this salad rape hollowed out to form a nest around a smaller pile of finely grated carrot. Top the carrot with finely chopped shallot and some peanuts and garnish with any leaf salad – such as sprigs of parsley, corn salad, land cress and rocket.

DECEMBER

A head of endive broken up and mixed with a small can of pineapple pieces that have been well drained and some sprigs

170

of watercress or a handful of land cress leaves. Garnish with small wedges of tomato.

Shredded 'Sugar Loaf' chicory mixed with a bunch of land cress leaves and a sliced half cucumber with the skin left on. Serve sliced baked beetroot garnished with chopped parsley in a separate dish.

A bed of salad rape topped by a mixture of grated apple, onion and celeriac plus a carton of natural cottage cheese. This is best served on individual plates and looks good garnished with chopped prunes.

Chinese cabbage finely shredded for the base with just a little grated 'Mino Early' white winter radish stirred in for extra flavour. Top the blend with a mixture of tinned garden peas and diced baked beetroot. Garnish with chopped chives.

Shredded 'Sugar Loaf' chicory mixed with a sliced banana and a handful of walnut halves. Garnish with sprigs of watercress.

On each individual plate, two lettuce leaves topped by a chopped unpeeled apple, small cubes of Cheddar cheese and about eight chopped filberts. If you like a sweet flavour, add a few whole raisins to each salad.

Rub a salad bowl with garlic, and mix together shredded Chinese cabbage, one red and one green unpeeled sliced apples (dipped in lemon juice to prevent browning) and the best part of a head of green celery chopped quite small. Garnish with half a dozen small whole cooked prunes.

On each plate, two cabbage leaves laid one in the other to form a saucer. In this, place half a 'Doyenne du Comice' pear that has been peeled, cored and dipped in lemon juice to prevent discolouring. Surround the pear half with a mixture of natural cottage cheese and diced red pepper. Garnish with small sprigs of watercress.

Tear up one of the heartless cabbage lettuce sold in the shops in midwinter and toss together with a handful of rocket, another of chop suey green leaves and two sliced pickled onions. Garnish the bowl with segments from two satsumas.

A punnet of salad rape mixed with a handful of land cress and another of corn salad arranged round the sides of a salad bowl that has first been rubbed with garlic. In the centre, pile some chopped sticks of green celery and half a 'China Rose' radish sliced wafer thin. Garnish with tiny sprigs of parsley.

A salad made from shredded Chinese cabbage mixed with the uncommon blanched stems of the Japanese parsley (Mitsuba) and the Mizuna form of Japanese greens with fringed leaves and white stalks, both chopped small. Stir in some chopped leaves of the garlic-flavoured Chinese leeks (chives) and a few chop suey green leaves, then garnish with a well-drained can of mandarin orange segments.

A base of finely shredded red cabbage mixed with a small finely chopped onion, topped by a pile of mixed grated apple and raw parsnip. Garnish with just a suggestion of chopped winter savory leaves, or other herb.

Cropping Plan for a Small Plot

When preparing a cropping plan for a garden, it is best to divide the area into three so that rotation of crops can be practised to avoid a build up of pest and disease problems and make full use of all plant foods. Plants with similar needs are grouped together in a section and over the three years of the rotation the sections are moved on until each type of crop has been grown on each part of the plot. In the fourth year the rotation begins again.

In the first year, the section intended for peas, beans and other crops that need similar conditions is deeply dug and generously fed in winter with farmyard manure or some other bulky organic material. These crops and the same treatment will go on to the next section in the second year and then on further to the end of the plot in the third year.

In the first year, the middle section intended for the brassicas is fed only with fertilisers, but if soil is at all acid is given a dressing of lime during winter. In the second year these crops go on to the bottom section and in the third year move to the top.

In the first year, the bottom end of the plot is used for root crops and others with similar needs and is fed only with fertilisers. These crops go on to the top of the plot next year and in the third year are grown on the middle section.

Perennial herbs are better grown in some other part of the garden, but parsley and annuals – like sweet basil and chervil – can fit into the rotation. Leaf salads and seed leaf mustard and cress can be fitted into small areas between other crops, while radishes can be sown in very short rows every few weeks through the season where space is available. Use of cloches is important to extend the season and protect half-hardy crops in late spring and summer.

Through the season, a pinch of lettuce seed can go in every three weeks or so and half-a-dozen plants be put out wherever there is a bit of space between crops. Loose leaf lettuce, in particular, is very economical of space.

Section 1 – manured	double row runner beans sown $\frac{1}{2}$ April under cloches/$\frac{1}{2}$ late May in open, as follow on to cloched lettuce planted in March	
	$\frac{1}{2}$ row ridge cucumbers planted May; train up netting to save space	$\frac{1}{2}$ row sweet peppers planted under cloches early June. Precede with radish, mustard and cress
	lettuce sown in two $\frac{1}{2}$ rows in open March and April; follow July by $\frac{1}{2}$ row each endive and Chinese cabbage	
	$\frac{1}{2}$ broad row spring onions sown March	$\frac{1}{2}$ row pickling onions sown March
	$\frac{1}{2}$ row tomatoes planted May	$\frac{1}{2}$ double row celery planted early June

Section 2 – fertilisers	$\frac{1}{2}$ row summer cabbage planted March; follow by lettuce sown June	$\frac{1}{2}$ row 'Minicole' cabbage planted late April
? lime	dwarf Brussels sprouts plants (12) put in late May	
	row savoy plants (12)	
	row – $\frac{1}{2}$ 'Pentland Brig' kale (6); $\frac{1}{2}$ 'Purple Sprouting' broccoli (6)	plant July; precede by broad beans, early peas, early potatoes
	row – $\frac{1}{2}$ Dutch white cabbage; $\frac{1}{2}$ red cabbage	

Section 3 – fertilisers	row cloches $\frac{1}{2}$ triple row carrots sown March, $\frac{1}{2}$ double row beetroot sown March; follow in July with 'White Sprouting' broccoli plants (4), late cauliflower plants (8)	
	row maincrop carrots sown early June	
	row long beet sown late April	

$\frac{1}{2}$ row globe beet sown June

$\frac{1}{2}$ row spinach beet or Swiss chard sown June

$\frac{1}{2}$ row dandelions sown May

$\frac{1}{2}$ row lettuce sown May; follow by spring onions sown late August

row chicory sown late June/ early July

$\frac{1}{2}$ row parsley sown March

$\frac{1}{2}$ row Alpine strawberries planted May

Area: approximately 30 ft x 24 ft

Chart of Recommended Varieties

Code

B   Blanch
C   Cover with cloches
H   Harvest
P   Plant or transplant
Pc   Plant or transplant under cold glass or plastic
Pg   Plant or transplant in gentle heat
S   Sow in open
Sc   Sow under cold glass or plastic
Sg   Sow in gentle heat
U   Use from store

	Jan.	Feb.	March	April	May	June	July	Aug.	Sept.	Oct.	Nov.	Dec.
Lettuce:												
'Fortune', 'Suzan', 'Little Gem'	Sg	Sg,Sc	Pc	H——————H								Sg
			Sc,S——————————S									
					H——————————————H							
'Barcarolle', 'Lobjoits Green', 'Continuity'				S——————S								
					H————————————————H							
'Sigmahead'			Sc,S——————————S									
					H——————————————H							
'Windermere', 'Webbs Wonderful'					S——————S							
						H——————————H						
'Avondefiance'						S——————S C————————C						
							H————————————————H					
'Grand Rapids', 'Salad Bowl', 'Deep Red'						S——————S						
							H——————————H					
'Kwiek'									S—S Pc H—H			

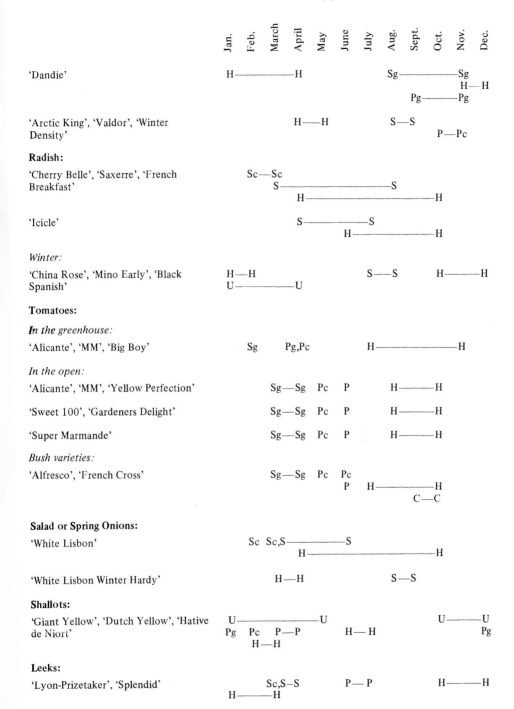

Appendix 2

	Jan.	Feb.	March	April	May	June	July	Aug.	Sept.	Oct.	Nov.	Dec.
'Dandie'	H————————H							Sg————————Sg				
											H—H	
									Pg————Pg			
'Arctic King', 'Valdor', 'Winter Density'				H——H				S—S				
										P—Pc		

Radish:

'Cherry Belle', 'Saxerre', 'French Breakfast'	Sc—Sc											
	S————————————————S											
	H————————————————————H											

| 'Icicle' | | | | S————————S | | | | | | | | |
| | | | | H————————————H | | | | | | | | |

Winter:

| 'China Rose', 'Mino Early', 'Black Spanish' | H—H | | | | | | S—S | | H————H | | | |
| | U————————U | | | | | | | | | | | |

Tomatoes:

In the greenhouse:

| 'Alicante', 'MM', 'Big Boy' | Sg | | Pg,Pc | | | | H————————————H | | | | | |

In the open:

'Alicante', 'MM', 'Yellow Perfection'			Sg—Sg	Pc	P		H————H				
'Sweet 100', 'Gardeners Delight'			Sg—Sg	Pc	P		H————H				
'Super Marmande'			Sg—Sg	Pc	P		H————H				

Bush varieties:

'Alfresco', 'French Cross'			Sg—Sg	Pc	Pc						
					P	H————————H					
						C—C					

Salad or Spring Onions:

'White Lisbon'			Sc	Sc,S————————S							
				H————————————————H							
'White Lisbon Winter Hardy'			H—H				S—S				

Shallots:

'Giant Yellow', 'Dutch Yellow', 'Hative de Niort'	U————————————U								U————U		
	Pg	Pc	P—P		H—H						Pg
		H—H								

Leeks:

| 'Lyon-Prizetaker', 'Splendid' | | | Sc,S–S | | P—P | | | H————H | | |
| | H————————H | | | | | | | | | |

	Jan.	Feb.	March	April	May	June	July	Aug.	Sept.	Oct.	Nov.	Dec.
Onions:												
Sets:												
'First Early'						H	—	HU—U	P	—	P	
'Sturon', 'Stuttgarter Giant'	U		P	P — U				H	H	U	—	U
Pickling:												
'The Queen', 'Paris Silverskin'	U	U	S	S				H	H	U	—	U
Cucumber:												
Indoor:												
'Femspot', 'Pepinex 69'			Sg	Sg	Pg / Pc	Pg / Pc	H	—	—	H		
Outdoor:												
'Burpee Hybrid', 'Perfection King of the Ridge', 'Kyoto', 'Crystal Apple', 'Amslic'				Sc / Sg	Sc / Sg / Pc / P	Pc / H	—	—	—	H		
Beetroot:												
'Avon Early', 'Boltardy'		Sc	Sc / S		H	—	S	—	H			
'Detroit', 'Cylindra', 'Formanova'	U	U			S	—	S / H	—	—	H	U	U
'Cheltenham Green Top', 'Long Blood Red', 'Covent Garden'	U	—	U	S	S						U	U
'Little Ball'						S	—	S	H	H		
'Burpee's Golden Beet', 'Albina Vereduna' ('Snowhite')					S	—	S	H	—	H		
Carrot:												
'Amsterdam Forcing'		Sc	Sc / S	S	H	H						
'Nantes-Tip Top'				Sc,S	—	H	S	—	—	H		
'Chantenay Red Cored', 'Kundulus'	U	—	U	S	—	—	S	H	—	H	U	U
Celery:												
'Golden Self-Blanching', 'American Green'				Sg	Sg / P	P		H	—	H		
'Solid White'. 'Giant Pink'	H	H	Sg	Sg	P						H	H

Appendix 2

	Jan.	Feb.	March	April	May	June	July	Aug.	Sept.	Oct.	Nov.	Dec.
Celeriac:												
'Globus', 'Jose'	H	H	Sg	Sg		P					H	H
Chicory:												
'Witloof'	B	B			S						B	B
	H	H										H
'Sugar Loaf', 'Crystal Head', 'Winter Fare', 'Snowflake'	C	C				S	S			H		H
	H	H										
'Red Verona'	H	H				S	S					H
Brussels Sprouts:												
'Peer Gynt'	H	Sc	S			P	P		H			H
'Citadel', 'Perfect Line', 'Rubine'	H		H	S	S	P	P				H	H
Broccoli:												
'White Sprouting', 'Purple Sprouting'		H			H							
				S	S	P		P				
Kale:												
'Pentland Brig'	H			H	S	P						
Cabbage:												
'Hispi', 'Golden Acre Progress', 'May Express'	Sg	Sg	S	P	P	H			H			
		Sc	Pc									
'Minicole'			S		S							
						P	P	H			H	
'Niggerhead'				S	S	P	P		H			H
'Holland Winter White'	U		U	S		P			H	H		U
Savoy:												
'Best of All'				S		P			H			H
'January King', 'Aquarius', 'Avon Coronet'	H	H		S	S	P	P				H	H
Spring Cabbage:												
'April', 'Offenham Spring Bounty', 'Spring Hero'					H		H	S	S	P	P	
Cauliflower:												
'Angers No. 2 – Westmarsh Early'				H	S	S	P	P				
'Angers No. 2 – Snow White'					H	S	P	P				
'Walcheren Winter-Birchington'				H	H S	P						

Appendix 2

	Jan.	Feb.	March	April	May	June	July	Aug.	Sept.	Oct.	Nov.	Dec.
'Walcheren Winter-Manston'					H S		P					

Chinese Cabbage:

	Jan.	Feb.	March	April	May	June	July	Aug.	Sept.	Oct.	Nov.	Dec.
'Sampan', 'Nagoaka', 'Tip Top No. 12', 'Che-foo', 'Market Pride'	H						S——S		H————H			

Endive:

	Jan.	Feb.	March	April	May	June	July	Aug.	Sept.	Oct.	Nov.	Dec.
'Moss Curled'						S——S	B————B					
								H————————H				
'Batavian Broad-leaved'	H					S————S		B———B				
									H—H			

Sweet Peppers:

	Jan.	Feb.	March	April	May	June	July	Aug.	Sept.	Oct.	Nov.	Dec.
'Early Prolific', 'Goldstar', 'Yellow Lantern', 'Twiggy', 'Triton'				Sg————Sg								
				Pc--Pc	H————————H							

List of Stockists for Seeds/Plants

Where a stockist has a more specialised list, this is indicated below.

P. Bakker (of Hillegom, Holland)
PO Box 120
Preston PR1 4BR

Chris Bowers   Fruit
Whispering Trees Nursery
Wimbotsham
Norfolk PE34 8QB

Chiltern Seeds   Oriental
Bortree Stile
Ulverston
Cumbria LA12 7PB

Samuel Dobie and Son Ltd
Upper Dee Mills
Llangollen
Clwyd LL20 8SD

The Herb Garden   Herbs
Cae-Rhos Lligwy
Brynteg
Tynygongl
Anglesey
Gwynedd
N Wales

S.E. Marshall and Co. Ltd
Wisbech
Cambs. PE13 2RF

Appendix 3

Bryan Mitton Seeds Ltd
Quadring
Spalding
Lincs. PE11 4PW

Ken Muir   Fruit and
Honeypot Farm   vegetable plants
Weeley Heath
Clacton-on-Sea
Essex CO16 9BJ

Suffolk Herbs   Herbs
Sawyers Farm
Lt. Cornard
Sudbury
Suffolk

Suttons Seeds Ltd
Hele Road
Torquay
Devon TQ2 7QJ

Thompson and Morgan Ltd
London Road
Ipswich
Suffolk IP2 0BA

Unwins Seeds Ltd
Histon
Cambridge
Cambs. CB4 4LE

Index

Index

Index

185

Index